At Issue

I Volunteerism

DI056863

Other Books in the At Issue Series:

At Issue

Volunteerism

Gary Wiener, Book Editor

GREENHAVEN PRESS

An imprint of Thomson Gale, a part of The Thomson Corporation

Detroit • New York • San Francisco • New Haven, Conn. • Waterville, Maine • London

Christine Nasso, *Publisher*
Elizabeth Des Chenes, *Managing Editor*

© 2008 The Gale Group.

For more information, contact:
Greenhaven Press
27500 Drake Rd.
Farmington Hills, MI 48331-3535
Or you can visit our Internet site at http://www.gale.com

ISBN-13: 978-0-7377-3888-9 (hardcover)
ISBN-10: 0-7377-3888-X (hardcover)
ISBN-13: 978-0-7377-3889-6 (pbk.)
ISBN-10: 0-7377-3889-8 (pbk.)

Library of Congress Control Number: 2007933682

Contents

Introduction

Future historians may well date the beginning of the twenty-first century as occurring on September 11, 2001. This historic date marking the terrorist attacks on New York City and Washington, DC, has also proven to be a watershed date for American volunteerism. In 1997, President Clinton's call for "a nation of volunteers" had little practical effect, "barely caus-[ing] a blip in the number of people volunteering," as Brian McGrory wrote in the *Boston Globe*. Yet four years later America's response to the 9/11 attacks took the form of massive outpourings of charitable donations and increased volunteerism. Shortly following the attacks, in his State of the Union address in January 2002, President George W. Bush called upon all Americans to dedicate themselves to public service, urging the average American to devote 4,000 hours to volunteerism over the course of a lifetime. He also called for the establishment of the USA Freedom Corps, an organization that would function under the executive branch of government to organize and fund volunteer services throughout the country. "Americans have always believed in an ethic of service," Bush said. "Americans serve others because their conscience demands it, because their faith teaches it, because they are grateful to their country and because service brings rewards much deeper than material success." Bush also believed that volunteerism could aid homeland security, as every citizen needed to be an additional set of eyes and ears for the government. "If people want to fight terror, do something kind for a neighbor, join the USA Freedom Corps, love somebody, mentor a child, stand up to evil with acts of goodness and kindness," Bush said.

Bush's words could hardly seem more innocuous, and yet they immediately came under fire from those on both the political right and left. Writing for the conservative Web site

NewsMax.com, Miguel A. Faria Jr. labeled the new program "compassionate fascism," stating, "When National Service . . . is directed by the State, it easily becomes perverted into compulsory service, regardless of the purported good intentions behind it. And if it is compulsory, then it's not freely exercised or given charitably, but required in other words, obligatory. . . . It is not American, or voluntary, or anything remotely associated with our legacy of freedom." The political left was equally suspicious, if on different grounds. Bush had urged ordinary citizens to report incidents of suspicious activity under what Jeremy Lott called "a potential ticking civil-liberties time bomb known as the Terrorist Information and Prevention System, or Operation TIPS for short." Lott added, "The TIPS Web site explains that the pilot program, which will be slowly 'phased in across the country,' will enlist the assistance of 'millions of American workers who, in the daily course of their work, are in a unique position to see potentially unusual or suspicious activity in public places.' These 'volunteers' will become the eyes and ears of the federal government—the first line of defense against an invisible terrorist threat." Many liberals wondered if Bush's new program would devolve into nothing more than, to quote blogger Steve Himmer, a "national system for paranoid nuts to report neighbors they don't like."

Whatever the cause, whether the 2001 terrorist attacks, Bush's call for increased public service, or simply the public's interest in "doing the right thing," volunteerism has become fashionable in the early twenty-first century. "Following the terrorist attacks of September 11, 2001, we've seen a tremendous increase in volunteer service among Americans," said Desiree T. Sayle, director of USA Freedom Corps. Volunteerism rose among Americans by nearly 12 percent from 2002 to 2005, according to a study done by the Points of Light Foundation. As Joe D. Jones wrote in 2005, "Volunteering is on the upswing in America. That's an uplifting tidbit of news amid all the disturbing reports on the economy, state budget and the stress of fighting the war in Iraq." To prove his assertion, one need look no further than the deluge of voluntary support that followed each major domestic or international tragedy in the early 2000s: The tsunami in East Asia and hurricane Katrina in the southern United States are two prominent examples where tragedy led to world-wide volunteer and charitable efforts.

One group that has displayed a large increase in volunteerism has been the youth of America, particularly students. According to Gail Mulkeen, District Career Internship and Service Coordinator for the Pittsford Central School District in upstate New York, "Through many federal, state, and local initiatives, student service to others has become increasingly promoted and supported throughout the country." Critics have charged that many students, especially at the high school level, may not be truly invested in volunteerism, but instead use public service simply to pad their resumes for college. Mulkeen sees just the opposite effect, however. She notes that while her school district does not mandate voluntary service, once students become engaged in public service, they get hooked: "Often they say, 'I was told I should do community service and now I want to do more—it has made me feel helpful and I am glad I did it.'"

With the increase in volunteerism has come increased scrutiny, as critics wonder whether all of this volunteer manpower is being directed toward the truly needy, or if it is just a feel-good effort designed to help those who "have" feel less guilty by helping the "have-nots." Some critics also claim that the lion's share of volunteer hours being logged by suburbanites is directed toward organizations such as museums, scouting, and the like and not toward solving complex societal issues such as poverty. As one volunteer organizer has bluntly stated: "Volunteer work is great, but it is very inefficient and can seldom do the job as well as a paid staff. That's no rap on volunteers, who [do] a terrific job. That's just reality."

Such criticisms have led to a call for increased governmental regulation of volunteerism under the auspices of federal programs such as AmeriCorps, USA Freedom Corps, and the Peace Corps. But critics of these programs are plenty. Senator Rick Santorum once dismissed the government sponsored AmeriCorps as a program "for hippie kids to stand around a campfire holding hands and singing 'Kumbaya' at the taxpayer expense."

Far from being a subject about which everyone can agree, volunteerism has occasioned complex and spirited debates regarding who should volunteer, where and when they should volunteer, and who should be the recipient of services. With studies showing that approximately one-third of Americans engage in some documented form of volunteerism, these questions are not likely to go away any time soon. The authors in *At Issue: Volunteerism* discuss the important role that volunteerism plays in everyday life and the issues it will continue to raise in American society.

1

Voluntary Public Service Is Superior to Mandatory Service

Alan W. Dowd

Alan W. Dowd is director of the Hudson Institute in Indianapolis where he researches U.S. foreign policy, civil society, and philanthropy. His articles have appeared in World & I, American Enterprise, American Outlook, National Review Online, American Legion Magazine, *and other national publications.*

Public service is a difficult concept to define because it can take so many different forms. Almost any type of effort that aids the public at large can be classified as public service. In the United States, a country founded on individualism, getting people to volunteer to work together to provide public service is not always easy. Many Americans resist government interference in volunteerism and resent any notions of mandatory service. In the twentieth-century, various U.S. presidents have instituted nationwide programs, such as the Peace Corps and Americorps, to provide large-scale non-mandatory volunteer opportunities. While these programs have many strengths, they can discourage people from taking the initiative to find their own ways to help their communities. Public service works best when it is not government mandated, but when people find their own way to best serve others.

There is a consensus in the United States that a key ingredient of maintaining a good society is involving Americans in service to something greater than themselves. The

Alan W. Dowd, "A Nation of Servants: Defining Public Service for the Twentieth Century," *The World & I*, January 2004, pp. 280–293. Copyright 2004 News World Communications, Inc. Reproduced by permission.

Founding Fathers believed it. Indeed, many of them sacrificed their lives—and, most of them, their wealth—for the greater cause of America's independence and nationhood. President John F. Kennedy awoke a generation with the phrase, "Ask not what your country can do for you; ask what you can do for your country." Some three decades later, President Bill Clinton declared, "Service is the spark to rekindle the spirit of democracy in an age of uncertainty." In the wake of the terrorist attacks on Washington and Manhattan, President George W. Bush challenged the American people to make "a commitment to service in [their] own communities. . . . Serve your country by tutoring or mentoring a child, comforting the afflicted, housing those in need of shelter and a home."

The U.S. Constitution begins with the phrase "We the people," not "I the individual."

Yet from the very beginning, the American people have valued the individual and rewarded individualism. After all, this is where the Pilgrims fled to find religious and political independence, the "Don't tread on me" flag once waved, homesteaders and frontiersmen daily redrew the borders of a nation, and the cowboy rode off into the sunset alone. Here free enterprise reigns and seemingly everyone is or once was an entrepreneur. As [nineteenth-century French writer] Alexis de Tocqueville concluded in *Democracy in America*, arguably the most insightful assessment of the American character ever written, "Individualism is a novel expression . . . a mature and calm feeling." The problem with individualism, according to de Tocqueville, is that it "saps the virtues of public life [and] in the long run . . . is absorbed in downright selfishness."

What was true in the early nineteenth century remains true in the twenty-first. Unbridled individualism seems to have eaten away at that all-important connective tissue between employees and employers, shareholders and executives, neighbors and neighborhoods, citizens and government, old and young. Instead of shared values and common responsibilities, there is a demand for rights and entitlements, a selfish competition to acquire and amass, to consume and claim. Talk of public service is often dismissed as quaint. Indeed, as the National Commission on the Public Service concluded in January 2003, "The notion of public service, once a noble calling, proudly pursued by the most talented Americans of every generation, draws an indifferent response from today's young people and repels many of the country's leading private citizens."

However, there remains a pull in the other direction, an undercurrent of cooperation and community that often redirects America's individualist impulse. This ebb and flow has always existed and was grafted into the very marrow of the United States: Although America's founding document was a declaration of *independence*, arguing that each person has a right to life, liberty, and the pursuit of his own happiness, the U.S. Constitution begins with the phrase "We the people," not "I the individual."

The challenge today, as in Jefferson and Madison's day, as in Kennedy's, is to strike a balance between these two competing forces—and to do so without expanding the size and scope of government any further. A first step in that direction is to recognize that anyone can participate in public service.

Defining Public Service

It may be helpful to define what public service is before considering how it contributes to a good society. Public service is both more and less than working for some government agency or winning an election. That's because serving the public demands more than simply taking an oath or wearing a uniform. Paradoxically, authentic public service doesn't require a citizen to enlist in the military, run for office, or join the Peace Corps. For that matter, it doesn't require a person to be a citizen: There are 31,000 foreign nationals serving in the U.S. armed forces. In fact, as the *Wall Street Journal* reported [in 2003], some of the very first American troops to die in Iraq weren't Americans at all, but rather immigrants such as Marine Corporal Jose Antonio Gutierrez from Guatemala.

Some expressions of public service are obvious: elective or judicial office, military service, national service programs. Some are not so obvious. The schoolteacher, Social security official, police officer or deputy sheriff, precinct committeeman, librarian, and juror are all public servants, whether we notice them or not.

So what is a good definition for public service? A dictionary entry points us in the right direction: Public service is simply "a service rendered in the public interest." By that definition, virtually anyone can be a public servant—no matter what his station in life.

If an action promotes the public good or meets the public's needs, it is public service. If it promotes something else or meets only private needs, it is something less than public service—no matter who is performing it.

This expansive definition calls to mind Justice Potter Stewart's wry observation on obscenity: "I know it when I see it." In the same way, public service may not be easily defined, but we know it when we see it.

New National Service Programs

Simply put, perhaps our concept of public service—focused as it is on government and politics—is too narrow. Consider the heroes of Flight 93 [on September 11, 2001], who died so that hundreds or thousands of other Americans might live. They weren't soldiers or statesmen, but they certainly served the public. Just as September 11 taught us that war is no longer something fought "over there," it should have reminded us that public service is not something performed exclusively by public officials, people in uniform, or politicians. It's something that every American can—and arguably should—do, which may explain Washington's numerous attempts to create and enlarge national-service programs.

Seventy Years of Federal Programs

Today, there are bills working their way through Congress that would create a National Youth Service Day, modernize the Peace Corps, revamp and streamline the well-known Ameri-Corps program, reorganize all federal service programs, form a civilian-service corps styled after "the best aspects of military service," [according to the Call to Service Act of 2003] and enlarge AmeriCorps. As the Corporation for National and Community Service details in its "History of National Service," this is nothing new: In 1910, U.S. philosopher William James called for the "conscription of the whole youthful population to form for a certain number of years a part of the army enlisted against nature." Twenty-three years later, FDR's [Franklin Delano Roosevelt] Civilian Conservation Corps did just that.

What the post-FDR government service programs lacked in utopian rationale, they made up for in sheer numbers. [President John F.] Kennedy created the Peace Corps in 1961 to deploy young Americans around the world on humanitarian missions. Not to be outdone, President Lyndon Johnson established VISTA, the National Teacher Corps, JobCorps, and other military-sounding organizations to wage his war on poverty. The Youth Conservation Corps was formed in 1970, followed by the Young Adult Conservation Corps in 1978. In the 1980s, Campus Outreach Opportunity League, Youth Service America, and other organizations were founded at the local level to attract young people to service. By 1990, President George H. W. Bush had launched the federal Points of Light Foundation and opened the Office of National Service inside the White House. Clinton commissioned the first 20,000 AmeriCorps workers in 1994. By the time he left office, some

200,000 Americans had participated in the program—at a cost to taxpayers of about $15,000 each.

Service During World War II and Now

Proponents of government-centered service programs are quick to argue that Americans are too self-centered to think about others, too oblivious and distracted to care about their country, too soft to sacrifice, that we lack the inclination to serve which characterized earlier generations. At first glance, they appear to be right: During World War II, my grandfathers and their generation marched off to Africa, Europe, and the Pacific's mosaic of islands and reefs. Some 400,000 of them never returned. On the home front, the wives, sweethearts, and sisters of America's fighting men served their country by donating metal and tin, giving up their nylon stockings, making do with bald tires and meatless Mondays, rationing gasoline, and forming an army of their own to operate the country's armament factories.

In the war on terror, by contrast, Uncle Sam hasn't made any such demands of the American people. In fact, during those first months after the attacks on Manhattan and the Pentagon, as the economy staggered, Bush urged Americans to "visit Disney World and America's other vacation spots." Congress passed an array of wartime tax cuts to prime the pump of American consumerism. Automakers, hotels, and airlines offered enticing packages to pry open our wallets and "keep America moving." What's more, there's no military draft; there's not even a push to recruit more troops. Service to country seems like little more than a punch line.

Nevertheless, post–September 11 America is not all that different from post–Pearl Harbor America. Consider a collection of World War II–era polling data unearthed by *American Enterprise* magazine. In 1942, after a year of fighting, only 23 percent of Americans said they had volunteered for civilian defense programs. In 1944, 66 percent of Americans said their fellow citizens weren't taking the war seriously enough, and 45 percent said they went about their business as if there were no war at all. In 1945, fully 64 percent of Americans said they had not made any real sacrifice for the war. [Derek] Leebaert [in *The Fifty-Year Wound*] adds, "After two years of fighting, nearly a third of the country did not know that the Philippines had fallen, and twice that many had never heard of the Atlantic Charter."

Voluntary Service Is Good Service

The purpose here is not to smear the "golden age" of service, sacrifice, and civic patriotism but rather to put things in perspective. Americans are individualistic and somewhat distrustful of government by nature. Hence, they don't flock to government-service programs. When government stays out of the way, however, they do serve and sacrifice for each other. As de Tocqueville observed, it is freedom itself that "leads a great number of citizens to value the affection of their neighbors and their kindred, perpetually brings men together, and forces them to help one another in spite of the propensities that sever them."

Perhaps the greatest social service that can be rendered by anybody to this country and to mankind is to bring up a family.

According to the eminent nonprofit scholar Richard Cornuelle, Americans have always wanted a nation that is both free and good. Writing in his landmark work, *Reclaiming the American Dream*, he notes that "our founders took pains to design a government with limited power, and then carefully scattered the forces which could control it." That would help nurture freedom. To promote a good society, "We developed a genius for solving common problems. People joined together in bewildering combinations to found schools, churches, opera houses, co-ops, hospitals, to build bridges and canals, to help the poor."

Our ancestors were committed to living independent lives, but to survive and thrive they also had to be interdependent. The result was, in a sense, a nation of servants.

According to Cornuelle, "The service motive is at least as powerful as the desire for profit or power." Like the profit motive, it can be curbed or encouraged by external forces: Just as burdensome tax policies, corruption, and regulations can stifle an individual's desire to make a profit, the government's co-opting of *public service* can stifle an individual's desire to serve. In other words, if government does too much, it could have the effect of discouraging people from serving their neighbor and nation. It is basic human nature that when a neighbor's needs appear to be met, the desire to serve ebbs. People simply won't take an active part in their nation or their neighborhoods if someone or something else is already playing that role. If, as de Tocqueville argued, "personal interest is restrained when confronted by the sight of other men's misery," then the converse is true as well: Personal interest is unleashed when that misery or need is being met by something else, especially the state. Once unleashed, it grows into the selfishness that de Tocqueville feared and today's advocates of government-endorsed, taxpayer-financed national service are right to criticize.

Americans have combated this selfishness not with government but with a vast array of what de Tocqueville called associations and free institutions—nongovernment organizations that keep us connected to each other and keep the government at bay. These organizations remind us [as de Tocqueville wrote] "that it is the duty as well as the interest of men to make themselves useful to their fellow creatures." This is the essence of public service—to be useful to your fellow-man—and despite the smothering embrace of government, Americans continue to fulfill this duty.

An Army of Volunteers

According to studies conducted by the Independent Sector, a coalition of nonprofit groups, there are 1.6 million charities, social welfare organizations, and religious congregations in the United States. The number of American adults who volunteer in any given year ranges between 84 million and 110 million. Together, this army of volunteers works 15.5 billion man-hours a year, representing the equivalent of over 9 million full-time employees. Astonishingly, they aren't being induced or paid to serve; they are able to serve without any guidance from Washington; and they are more effective and far less expensive than their counterparts in government-run programs.

The evidence is all around us. Consider the Habitat for Humanity branch that builds homes for the homeless and hopeless, the church that delivers food to shut-ins, the law firm that does pro bono work for immigrants and paupers, the physicians group that quietly provides "charity care," the clinic that donates supplies to a school nurse's office, the foundation that helps build universities and hospitals, the business that partners with a community group to clean up a neighborhood, the Little League dads and Scout moms who teach values of good citizenship and hard work to the children in their care, or, for that matter, any parent. As the British progressive George Bernard Shaw concluded, "Perhaps the greatest social service that can be rendered by anybody to this country and to mankind is to bring up a family."

As the poet Robert Browning observed, "All service ranks the same with God."

All of these people and institutions serve the public in some significant way, and this is just the tip of the iceberg.

The line between public service and the private sector—indeed, between government and nongovernment service—is rapidly blurring, as faith-based organizations and corporations partner with federal, state, and local governments to provide goods and services that once were the sole responsibility of government.

For example, according to *Government Executive* magazine, the Pentagon is increasingly "hiring contractors to provide support behind the lines." Companies such as Brown and Root are based alongside U.S. forces throughout the Balkans. They repair vehicles, build barracks, operate convenience stores, manage 95 percent of the Army's rail lines and airfields, cook meals, wash laundry, and, in the words of one employee, "do everything that does not require us to carry a gun." *Government Executive* found that for every two troops deployed in the Balkans, there are three contractors. A little over a decade ago, by way of comparison, there was just one contractor for every one hundred troops in the Gulf. Today, there is one contractor for every ten troops in Iraq. Everywhere they are deployed, both the troops and the contractors are in harm's way, as a flurry of prewar attacks underscored last January [2003]. A civilian contractor based at Camp Doha in Kuwait was killed, another wounded, during the buildup.

The employees of these quasi-government organizations and government subcontractors are in a sense public servants. They may be public servants twice removed, but they're still serving the public.

Every American has the capacity and opportunity to serve something greater than self, and countless millions do so everyday. Sometimes they do so through government, but often they do not. If the goal is to maintain a good society, or to build a better society, then counteracting selfishness with service is indeed important. However, Washington does not need to pass new legislation, restart the draft, or create new programs to achieve that balance. In fact, rather than expanding programs, Washington needs to expand its definition of *public service*. As the poet Robert Browning observed, "All service ranks the same with God."

2

Our Government Should Be Involved in Public Service

Morton A. Kaplan

Morton A. Kaplan is a Professor Emeritus of political science at the University of Chicago. Until 2004, he served as editor-in-chief and publisher of The World & I, *a monthly magazine of politics, science, culture, and other global issues.*

Alan Dowd [author of the previous article] makes many valid points in his article on the value of freely given public service without government interference. However, there are many times when government regulation is a positive force to spur individual citizens to action on behalf of their country. The military draft, the Peace Corp, and Americorp are three instances where government regulation of voluntary services has worked. Rewarding volunteers in the form of payments or other benefits, contrary to Dowd's assertions, is a valuable way to coax otherwise reluctant volunteers into service. Most important, in the United States, volunteers for military or other service should come from all classes of society, including those wealthy individuals who have traditionally been able to avoid military service or other unpleasant government service. A country is strongest when all of its people, regardless of class, volunteer for service.

A lan Dowd has written a profound article that espouses the value of public service. I share with him an aversion to extreme demands for rights and entitlements in favor of a concept of shared values and commitments. I agree that restricting the concept of public service to government service is too narrow. However, although Dowd's broad definition of public service is correct, it tends to obscure the fact that some forms of service are more integral to social membership than others, a subject to which I shall return.

Although correctly stressing the value of voluntary decisions, Dowd carries this principle beyond practical limits. He even objects to the remission of government loans as recompense for service as a form of coercion. But coercion has an appropriate role in ensuring that important aspects of public service are carried out.

Forced Volunteerism Is Sometimes Necessary

There are many facets of public life in which voluntarism will not do. For instance, paying taxes is a form of public service as he broadly defines it. Yet when Illinois put a tax on personal property, virtually no one paid it because they thought many others would evade it. If the income tax were made voluntary, our armed services would not even be at the almost-useless European level. The face-to-face communities that allow volunteer fire forces to operate would not work in a large city.

Many who served in the Peace Corps and later in Ameri-Corps take pride in that service.

If the nation had not had a draft law during World War II, it never would have been able to place eleven million men under arms. When General Marshall permitted a relaxation of the draft at the end of the war, this produced riots in the Pacific Theater by troops who had fought the war and feared they would not be replaced. The subsequent rapid demobilization [discharge from military service] of the armed forces made the Soviet decision to permit the North Korean attack in 1950 a reasonable gamble.

Our troops in the Pacific consisted of poorly equipped, almost skeletal divisions when the Korean War broke out. Only when the draft was reinstituted was the United States able to preserve South Korea. Today, our troops in Iraq are stretched thin and our reservists are threatening to leave the reserves because of what they regard as excessive and unshared burdens. It is because the public will not accept a new draft that these unfair burdens are being placed upon those who do serve. This is doing damage to the country.

Paying Volunteers Can Work

Dowd calls remissions of loans to those who do serve organizations such as AmeriCorps a form of compulsion to which he objects. But the doctors who work for a time in underserved communities in return for remission of tuition help are doing something that is needed and that would not be done in the absence of this "compulsion." The same is true for those teachers who agree to work in underserved communities. Many who undergo this "compulsion" in fact take pride in these services.

But then is not all payment for all employment a form of compulsion in Dowd's terms? How does remission of tuition grants differ from other forms of payment? Do not most individuals take jobs only because they are paid to do so? And is not the government often, if not always, the best place to organize help for underserved communities on a systematic basis by providing benefits?

Many who served in the Peace Corps and later in AmeriCorps take pride in that service. Perhaps in the current climate of opinion, a draft for these agencies or even for the military services is not politically feasible. Although making such service compulsory would be counterproductive if the work became meaningless, instituting a year of service, with choice as to type of service, in the year after high school might institute a sense of pride and of commitment in those who served if they could see that good things resulted. For instance, with proper training AmeriCorps could be used in developing the brains of children of poor single mothers before significant damage is done to their ability to learn and become productive citizens.

Just as individual decisions have their place in society, group decisions and not just group values also have a place. Which method of decision is to be employed in a particular case cannot be determined in general. Only an evaluation related to the concrete circumstances of particular societies at particular times will turn out to be useful. What seems clear is that self-interest and community interest in contemporary American society are unbalanced. Dowd is right to object, but supporting AmeriCorps better than we do is also the right thing to do.

A strong nation with a strong sense of public service would be one in which individuals from all backgrounds would desire a period of service in the military . . .

All People, Regardless of Class, Should Serve the Public or All Classes of People Should Serve

It is a shame that a military draft is unfeasible, even though it might be counterproductive even if feasible, in the current state of social values. It is wrong that rich kids, except perhaps from a South in which military values are still strong, cannot be tempted by payments to enter military service when poor kids enter the service in many cases only because of this temptation. A nation in which we do not serve together in dangerous necessary tasks will not be as strong as a nation in which we do.

Dowd is right to point out how broad the concept of public service is, but some forms of service are more crucial to society than others. The heart of America is that it is in principle a classless society. Military service may be only one form of public service, but it is a crucial one. Except where conscience is involved, as in the case of pacifists, opting out should not be a choice that the rich can make so much more easily than the poor. Reinstituting the military draft may not be politically possible. It might become counterproductive even if possible. But it is not in principle wrong.

A strong nation with a strong sense of public service would be one in which individuals from all backgrounds would desire a period of service in the military, as do the Swiss, independently of payment and career training. In the absence of a strong sense of commitment that leads those from all backgrounds to volunteer for dangerous service in wars, a draft is desirable and may be necessary in some circumstances. It undermines the health and safety of a nation if those who serve feel that they have become dupes of the rich, the powerful, or the in-different.

3

The United States Does Not Need New Volunteer Agencies

Martin Hill

Martin Hill is editor of the San Diego Business Journal.

In the wake of the September 11, 2001, attacks on New York City and Washington, DC, President George W. Bush created the USA Freedom Corps, an organization to oversee volunteer efforts in the United States, particularly those dealing with national security; however, numerous volunteer groups, from the U.S. Coast Guard Auxiliary to the American Red Cross are already in place. These volunteer organizations are highly effective in supporting the government's response to crises, and it is not necessary to create new organizations to support them. The United States does not need more bureaucracy that will only confuse and slow down its response to crises. Instead, current volunteers need support and assurances that the time they devote to serving will not jeopardize their status in their regular jobs. President Bush could help this cause by urging businesses to be more supportive of volunteer efforts.

Dear Mr. President:

I applaud your recent call for more volunteerism among Americans, which you made in your State of the Union Address [in 2002]. However, I do not believe you need to establish a new agency—you call it the USA Freedom Corps—to oversee such volunteer efforts. Nor do I believe you need to

Martin Hill, "Volunteers: An Open Letter to the Prez.," *San Diego Business Journal*, vol. 23, March 4, 2002, p. 42. Copyright 2002 CBJ, L.P. Reproduced by permission.

establish a Citizen Corps for those wishing to help with homeland defense, or a Medical Reserve Corps to help with medical response in times of crisis.

In the immortal words of your father, "Been there. Done that." In other words, Mr. President, such groups already exist.

I speak from experience, Mr. President. I'm a volunteer.

Important Volunteer Agencies Are Already in Place

As a member of the U.S. Coast Guard Auxiliary, the civilian volunteer corps of the Coast Guard, and the San Diego County Sheriff's Search and Rescue (SAR) Bureau, I provide several hundred hours of volunteer service each year. The problem is, Mr. President, very few people know what valuable service such groups provide—particularly our employers.

For instance, most people know the Coast Guard Auxiliary as those people who teach free boating safety courses and offer safety inspections for recreational boats. Boating safety is, indeed, a high priority for the Auxiliary, but it's only one of several missions it performs.

During World War II, the Auxiliary provided the bulk of the manpower for port security operations and anti-submarine patrols in U.S. waters. Sixty years later, the Auxiliary is performing similar duties.

Since Sept. 11 [2001], Auxiliarists can be found on anti-terrorist security patrols in San Diego Bay at all hours, day and night, in good weather and bad, acting as the eyes and ears of the sadly undermanned active-duty Coast Guard.

Some Auxiliarists, such as myself, have been trained to active-duty standards and serve part-time aboard cutters, small boat stations, air stations, and marine safety offices. These Auxiliarists have also been serving on the front lines of homeland defense—for no pay.

In fact, Mr. President, in the first six weeks following the attacks in New York and Washington, Auxiliarists provided

12,000 hours of service in the San Diego area alone in support of Operation Noble Eagle, the nation's homeland defense initiative. Since Sept. 11, Auxiliary contributions in support of homeland defense are nearing 200,000 hours.

Like Auxiliarists, the volunteers serving with the Sheriffs SAR Bureau work entirely without pay. Each member undergoes five months of training in the department's nationally renowned SAR Academy, learning search theory, man tracking, rappelling, medical aid, wilderness survival and much more.

After that, they join specialized units for further training. An emergency medical technician (basic), I belong [to] the SAR Bureau's medical unit.

On missions, members of the SAR Bureau are reinforced by the San Diego Mountain Rescue Team, another group of highly trained volunteers. Members of both units are on call 24 hours a day, seven days a week to search for lost hikers and hunters, recover plane crash victims and wandering Alzheimer's patients, evacuate homes in the path of wildfires, and hunt for missing children—most recently, young Danielle van Dam.

We also assist in law enforcement support operations. Each of us is also a registered With the California Office of Emergency Services as a state disaster worker, and can be mobilized for disaster aid anywhere in the state or the nation.

Groups like these exist in every county in the nation, Mr. President. And they're not alone.

Medical Reserve Corps and The Red Cross

For instance, your Medical Reserve Corps already exists. U.S. Public Health Service Disaster Medical Assistance Teams—comprsing volunteer medical professionals such as doctors, nurses, paramedics and EMTs—stand ready across the country to respond to the scene of disasters to bolster local medical services. San Diego's D-MAT CA-4, for instance, recently deployed to the Winter Olympics in Utah to provide medical backup if needed.

When the Twin Towers crumbled in New York on Sept. 11, Mr. President, another group of volunteers were activated to respond to the disaster—the Urban Search and Rescue Units. USAR teams, composed of medical personnel, construction experts and heavy equipment operators, are located in most large cities to provide heavy rescue assistance at disaster scenes. Volunteers from San Diego's USAR team, for example, spent three terrible weeks at the Twin Towers recovering bodies. Their only pay are memories that may never leave them in peace again.

Then there are Red Cross volunteers, Mr. President. Whatever some may say about the administrators of the American Red Cross, the volunteers in the field are the epitome of volunteerism. They're everywhere they could possibly be needed providing food, comfort and shelter.

Mostly recently, local Red Cross volunteers could be found at the Fallbrook wildfire, which swept across a large portion of North County. They also provided food and drink to those searching for the missing van Dam girl. One recent rainy day spent in the field with my sheriff's unit, soaked to the skin, my mood brightened significantly when given a warm meal by an equally drenched Red Cross volunteer.

Volunteers Trained to Aid Government Agencies

The list of volunteer groups doesn't stop here, Mr. President. The Federal Emergency Management Agency-sponsored Community Emergency Response Teams throughout the country— volunteer citizens trained to deal with disasters in their own neighborhoods.

Like the Coast Guard, the Air Force has its own corps of civilian volunteers, officially known as the U.S. Air Force Auxiliary, but commonly called the Civil Air Patrol. Even the National Guard has an auxiliary in the form of state militias and state military reserves—unpaid, uniformed volunteers who backfill when the Guard needs extra manpower.

We don't need new bureaucracies, Mr. President. The infrastructure for volunteerism exists.

And the list just keeps going on, Mr. President. Unpaid police reserves, volunteer firefighters and ambulance technicians, volunteer hospital workers—an endless cornucopia of volunteer opportunities.

Why do people volunteer? I believe my volunteerism stems from the same source that compelled me to enlist in the military—twice—and to become a journalist: my sister dropped me on my head when I was small. Others, however, have more altruistic motives—a sense of giving back to the community and the nation, not to mention the camaraderie of serving.

Current Volunteers Need Support

We don't need new bureaucracies, Mr. President. The infrastructure for volunteerism exists. We need only two things: money and the support of business.

This is what volunteers need most, Mr. President—time and the security of knowing that the time we spend serving our community and our nation won't jeopardize our livings.

Volunteer organizations are always in need of money. We volunteers pay for our uniforms and most of our equipment—to the tune of thousands of dollars. What we don't pay for comes from our parent organization or grants. Making more money available to these organizations would go much further to realizing your aim of increasing volunteerism than creating new organizations.

In addition, being a volunteer means being away from home a lot, not only for missions but training as well. It also means being away from work a lot. Without supportive employers, Mr. President, volunteers cannot succeed.

For three months following the Sept. 11 attacks, I stood duty every few days at my Coast Guard station, filling in until its manpower could be increased by the reassignment of activated reserves and regulars. The *[San Diego] Business Journal* supported me by matching each vacation day I took for duty with another day—saving me both vacation time and money.

This is what volunteers need most, Mr. President—time and the security of knowing that the time we spend serving our community and our nation won't jeopardize our livings. This is where we need your support.

Mr. President, you can do far more for volunteerism in this country by encouraging business support for our activities than by creating new agencies. By offering businesses incentives for giving employees time off for volunteer work, you could bolster the ranks of volunteers needed to serve America in this time of crisis.

This, Mr. President, is what the 80-plus million volunteers in America need from you.

Sincerely,
Martin Hill

4

USA Freedom Corps Is Working to Amass Volunteers

George W. Bush

George W. Bush is the 43rd President of the United States and founded the USA Freedom Corps in 2002 as a response to the September 11th 2001 attacks on New York City and Washington, DC.

Americans are blessed with freedom and prosperity, and these advantages create an obligation to help the less fortunate. USA Freedom Corps and organizations like it create the opportunity for Americans to serve their country through volunteerism. Americans have organized under the USA Freedom Corps to fight against terrorism and various natural disasters, and these efforts have helped numerous others. USA Freedom Corps is an umbrella program that successfully promotes such organizations as the Peace Corp and AmeriCorps and encourages nonprofit, faith-based, and community organizations to do their necessary volunteer work. USA Freedom Corps has enabled Americans to join together to work for causes greater than self and strengthen the United States as a whole.

Americans enjoy great liberty and prosperity, and with these blessings comes an obligation to reach out to those in need. Over the past 4 years, USA Freedom Corps has worked to rally America's armies of compassion and bring together individuals and organizations committed to volunteer service. More than 65 million people volunteered in 2005, an

George W. Bush, "Proclamation 7977—Fourth Anniversary of Freedom Corps, 2006," *Weekly Compilation of Presidential Documents*, vol. 42, no. 5, February 6, 2006, p. 143.

increase of 6.5 million since 2002. As we celebrate the fourth anniversary of USA Freedom Corps, we recognize the many Americans who have stepped forward to help others, and we underscore our commitment to serving our Nation and people around the world.

Combatting Terrorism, Tsunamis, and Hurricanes

USA Freedom Corps was created to build on the countless acts of service, sacrifice, and generosity that followed the terrorist attacks of September 11, 2001. In the wake of the devastating tsunami of 2004 and hurricanes of 2005, Americans have continued to demonstrate that the true strength of our Nation lies in the hearts and souls of our citizens. By reaching out to aid the victims of these tragedies, people across our country helped rebuild shattered lives and communities. Their acts of service again demonstrated that by loving our neighbors as ourselves, we can offer hope and healing to those who suffer.

USA Freedom Corps encourages and promotes the good work of nonprofit, faith-based, and community organizations.

USA Freedom Corps is dedicated to expanding volunteer service and extending the goodwill of the American people. To help support our communities, respond to crises at home, and spread compassion around the globe, USA Freedom Corps works to strengthen public service programs such as the Peace Corps, Senior Corps, AmeriCorps, and Citizen Corps USA. Freedom Corps encourages and promotes the good work of non-profit, faith-based, and community organizations. Through the President's Greeter Program and the President's Volunteer Service Award, USA Freedom Corps and the President's Council on Service and Civic Participation recognize Americans who have made serving their neighbors a central part of their lives. USA Freedom Corps has also created a comprehensive network of volunteer opportunities to help more Americans find ways to get involved in serving their communities.

Building a Culture of Service

Through USA Freedom Corps, my Administration will continue to build a culture of service, citizenship, and responsibility in our country. By working together for a cause greater than self, we can strengthen our Nation, one person, one neighborhood, and one community at a time.

Now, Therefore, I, George W. Bush, President of the United States of America, by virtue of the authority vested in me by the Constitution and laws of the United States, do hereby proclaim the Fourth Anniversary of USA Freedom Corps. I call upon the citizens of this great country to find ways to volunteer and help their fellow Americans. I commend the efforts of USA Freedom Corps and all those who have already answered the call to serve, and I encourage all Americans to donate their time, energy, and talents to the work ahead.

5

Volunteers Are Highly Effective if Used Properly

Athanassios (Ethan) Strigas

Athanassios (Ethan) Strigas is an assistant professor of Sports Management at Indiana State University. His academic interests focus on sport volunteerism, sport marketing and finance, sport diplomacy and policy development. Strigas has published articles in such journals as Sport Management International, International Sports Journal *and the* Journal of ICHPKR.

Current research in the field of sports and recreational volunteerism shows that volunteers are both effective and important to the community when properly employed. Volunteers contribute socially to society by increasing community cohesion, and they contribute monetarily because their efforts have an enormous financial benefit. For these reasons, it is essential that community groups attract a steady force of seasoned volunteers to supplement paid workers. Groups must target key factors that motivate volunteers if they wish to retain a maximum number of volunteer workers. Research studies on volunteerism can provide agencies with insight into how to retain their volunteers. Agencies wishing to attract volunteers should study current research and implement such studies in order to market themselves effectively to prospective volunteers.

Volunteer labor is extremely valuable to an organization because it provides its administrators with the ability to sustain services, expand the quantity, quality and diversity of

Athanassios (Ethan) Strigas, "Research Update: Making the Most of Volunteers," *Parks & Recreation*, vol. 41, April 2006, pp. 26–29. Reproduced by permission of the author.

these services, while keeping a project's budget within its pre-specified limits. For individuals associated with voluntary organizations, offering time, services and expertise helps increase self-esteem, facilitates new relationships, develops skills and abilities, reduces depression levels, and builds healthier attitudes about aging.

However, one of the predominant benefits of volunteering is a stronger sense of social and community cohesion. Communities that face challenging problems rely heavily on volunteer labor to overcome needs and difficulties, improve their public image and promote social harmony, understanding, equality and tolerance.

According to 2004 Bureau of Labor Statistics data collected for its monthly Current Population Survey, about 64.5 million (28 percent) of the population age 16 or older had volunteered for various organizations at least once during the previous year. This volunteer labor force spent a median of 52 hours on volunteer activities. Considering the estimated value of a volunteer hour is currently up to $17.55, it is obvious that volunteers have an enormous financial impact on the fabric of the U.S. society.

Who Volunteers and Why

People in the 35- to 44-year-old age bracket (34.2 percent of the U.S. population) were found to be the most likely to offer time and expertise in order to serve various social causes, among them the enhancement of park and recreation services. This group was followed closely by the 45- to 54-year-old group (32.8 percent) and the 55- to 64-year-old group (30.1 percent).The survey also discovered that teenagers demonstrated a relatively high volunteer rate (29.4 percent), which is attributed to the new emphasis in schools on volunteer activities.

The study also found Caucasians volunteer at higher rates than any other ethnic/racial group in the United States; part-time employees are more likely to participate in volunteer activities than full-timers; and married people volunteer at higher rates than people who are divorced, single or live with a partner.

Based on this data, and considering research reports on volunteerism for park and recreation agencies from countries that resemble the characteristics of the U.S. (i.e., Canada, Australia), the profile of the typical community sport volunteer is an individual between 34- and 45-years-old with a higher education degree, a full-time job and an annual income that exceeds $60,000. That person most likely has participated in organized sport activities in the past and was surrounded by people who volunteered.

Findings from the National Survey of Giving, Volunteering, and Participating also provide an interesting insight on this issue. The survey results seem to align themselves with results from generic studies in volunteerism regarding the predominant motives for volunteering services: time and expertise.

The survey found that volunteers for sport and recreation offer their assistance because they want to help a cause they believe in (94 percent), want to develop skills and acquire experiences in order to contribute to the leisure organization's cause (87 percent) and because someone they are affiliated with (significant others, children, etc.) is affected by the leisure organization and its programs (76 percent).

These results are greatly supported by a number of volunteerism studies on recreational sport events, conducted by Strigas and Jackson (2001, 2003). According to these studies, the primary motives for volunteering were because it was fun to volunteer services for recreational sport events; the volunteer wanted to help make the event a success; volunteering creates a better society; the volunteer wanted to put something back in my community; and volunteering makes the volunteer feel better about himself or herself.

Five Major Motivational Factors

Strigas (2001) has also proposed a motivational model that broadens the existing knowledge about the motives of volunteer labor in sport and recreation events. The study results advocate the existence of five major motivational factors that explain volunteerism.

The first factor is called "Social Functions of Leisure," which supports . . . [the] theory that volunteering is better conceptualized as a leisure choice. It involves motives related to the individual's needs for social interaction and interpersonal relationships, as well as motives related to the individual's need to relax or look into various leisure choices (i.e., "I wanted to relieve the stress and the tension of everyday life," "I wanted to develop relationships with others," "I wanted to discover new interests").

The second factor is labeled "Material" and involves motives that permit volunteers "to carry out a rational calculus of expected utility gain," in exchange for their services. These rewards can be material goods or services (some with a monetary value), or even social status that can easily be translated into a "reward" that carries a material value (i.e., "I wanted to make new contacts that might help my business or career.")

The third factor is called "Egoistic" and involves motives related to the individual's needs of self actualization, self-esteem, and achievement ("Volunteering makes me feel better about myself," "I wanted to help make the event a success").

The fourth factor is labeled "Purposive" and involves motives related to the desire of the volunteers to aid the leisure organization in the accomplishment of their goals, and contribute to the recreational sport event and the community ("I am genuinely concerned about the particular club I am serving," "I adhere to the organizational committee's specific goals").

The fifth factor is termed "External Influences" and assesses the extent to which volunteers donate time due to factors outside of their immediate control, like family traditions or decisions by significant others. ("My friends/family/ significant others are also volunteering," "I was asked by others to volunteer").

Recruiting More Volunteers

In her work, *A Profile of Community Sport Volunteers*, [A.] Doherty proposed a motivational model for volunteering that further supports the work of Strigas et. al. displayed above. That model identifies three levels of volunteer motives: a core motive that reflects altruism in volunteering, primary motives related to volunteer's personal needs and interests, and, lastly, social and personal development motives that constitute secondary motives for sport volunteering at the community level.

Recruiting and retaining volunteer labor are primary marketing problems.

Park and recreation administrators should also look at factors that discourage potential or existing volunteers from becoming involved. This raises a few questions: why don't people in the community volunteer their services for the leisure organization? Why don't existing volunteers volunteer more hours? And why do existing volunteers choose to discontinue offering services, time or expertise?

Research has provided some indications and potential answers to these questions. However, it is imperative to treat each leisure organization as a unique case. The most predominant answers indicate the volunteer had a poor previous experience with volunteering; the volunteer has a lack of time because family, work or other commitments; the volunteer had developed a false understanding of what was involved in his or her volunteer assignment; there was a perceived lack of skills and abilities on behalf of volunteers (or prospective volunteers); volunteers were disappointed in the way the leisure organization is functioning; increased demands on volunteers from volunteer coordinators; and the leisure organization may do a poor job in recruiting volunteers and lack a specific volunteer marketing plan (e.g. the agency does not ask people to volunteer, does not adequately communicate to them its mission and vision for the future, etc.).

The growing use of volunteer labor in different facets of everyday life creates a compelling need for people who are involved with leisure organizations, to review and re-evaluate the existing knowledge regarding volunteer activity. Recruiting and retaining volunteer labor are primary marketing problems. It is important for the park and recreation profession to develop the profile of the leisure and recreation volunteer. Agencies could use this knowledge to design their marketing efforts in a way that could appeal persuasively to this free labor during recruitment time.

Volunteers have an enormous financial impact on the fabric of U.S. society.

6

Volunteer Programs Enhance Corporate Effectiveness

Jill Elswick

Jill Elswick is associate editor of Employee Benefit News, *a Washington, DC-based monthly trade publication. She has covered topics such as consumer-driven health care, 401(k) advice and education, and elder care benefits. Elswick has previously served as interim editor of* Virginia Tech Magazine, *the alumni magazine of Virginia Polytechnic Institute and State University in Blacksburg, Virginia.*

Businesses that establish their own volunteer programs can reap important rewards, both for employees who participate and for the business itself. The key is for corporations to provide targeted volunteer opportunities, not merely random ones, which enhance worker skills as well as providing service to the community. Targeted volunteer opportunities allow employees to gain skills that make them more effective in their everyday jobs. For these programs to be most effective, however, volunteer efforts should not be mandated but should grow out of employee interests. If done correctly, genuine philanthropy and business success can coexist.

Asking not what their country can do for them, Americans would nevertheless like to know what employers can help them do for their country. And as more workers catch the spirit, employers are learning to apply business strategy to volunteerism benefits.

The advantages are multi-faceted, according to sponsors and civic leaders. By emphasizing opportunities for workers to grow their job skills through volunteer projects, strategic volunteerism rewards the company and the community.

In 2003, volunteer ranks grew to nearly 64 million, up four million from the previous year, according to the Bureau of Labor Statistics. With 36% of workers in 2003 reporting that their employer provides a formal volunteerism program—up from 29% in 2001, according to Walker Information—employers are helping spur the phenomenon.

Matching Skills and Volunteer Opportunities

Strategic volunteerism means finding where corporate values and skills meet, then matching those characteristics to the needs of local nonprofit organizations, explains Dave Remick, corporation services manager for Greater D.C. Cares, an organization that coordinates and promotes volunteer opportunities in the Washington, D.C. metro area.

"It's creating a partnership between the company and the nonprofit organization, thereby making a greater impact," Remick says.

For example, Dulles, Va.-based America Online, Inc., one of Greater D.C. Cares' corporate partners, launched AOL Tech-Corps as a chance for its technology professionals to upgrade the computer systems of nonprofit organizations. The arrangement not only helps the community but also builds the technical skills of AOL employees, saving the company thousands of dollars on training programs.

"You can paint a fence and mow a lawn, and those things are great and needed, but skills-based volunteering is a huge opportunity," observes Remick, who is preparing to launch an "HR Corps" of human resource professionals to assist D.C.-area nonprofit organizations with staffing challenges.

Other strategic volunteerism opportunities include executives serving on boards of directors, or "executive loan" programs in which professionals serve a full-time tour of duty with a nonprofit organization.

"The loaned executive program trains a junior-level person or mid-level manager for executive leadership by putting them into fundraising activities, speaking engagements, recruitment, event planning—you name it, they're doing it," says Remick.

Employee Volunteer Programs Are Valuable

Reed Dewey, director of corporate partnerships for the Points of Light Foundation, which was founded in 1990 by former President George Bush to promote volunteerism, says he's seeing rising interest in skills-based volunteerism.

"The foundation is bullish on employee volunteering to build skill and has been working in this area since it was founded," says Dewey, who describes three major components for "excellence" in workplace volunteering programs.

How can you become more effective in your current job? . . . We view many volunteer activities as wonderfully developmental. . . .

First, he says, companies must "acknowledge that employee volunteer efforts contribute to the achievement of business goals." Second, they must "commit to establish, support and promote an employee volunteer program that encourages the involvement of every employee and to manage that program like it's any other business function." Finally, they must "target workplace volunteering to focus on specific social problems in the community." Toy manufacturers and retailers, for example, might identify a need for playgrounds.

"Employee volunteer programs are not just a feel-good effort," Dewey says. "They really do add value, and the companies we work with tell us that."

He advises companies to take a hard look at corporate culture, get senior management buy-in, and determine time-off policies before implementing a volunteer program. He also suggests promoting collaboration across departments and divisions in developing the program. . . .

Volunteerism Can Fit in A Business Model

Seattle-based Safeco Insurance received an award for excellence in workplace volunteer programs from the Points of Light Foundation in 2002.

"We're in the business of providing service to people when they're having a bad day," says Allie Mysliwy, senior vice president of HR. "Part of our values is 'other-directedness.' It's a natural jump from helping people as part of our jobs to inside our community. Volunteerism really is aligned with our business model."

Volunteering should be just that. . . . It should be optional. Mandatory volunteering is an oxymoron.

One of Safeco's programs, called "Building Business Skills through Volunteerism," is tied to the employee development process.

"How can you become more effective in your current job? How can you become more effective for the job you want? We view many volunteer activities as wonderfully developmental," says Mysliwy.

Volunteerism helps employees "learn on the fly" and take new risks, he says. Safeco's employee Web site includes developmental resources related to volunteering; the company also runs a matching site through VolunteerMatch.org to help employees find opportunities specific to their interests.

Safeco gives employees paid time off to volunteer; managers determine how much time an employee can take. The company pays nonprofit organizations $10 for each hour an employee spends volunteering there. It also matches employee gifts.

Businesses Must Keep Programs Strictly Voluntary

Many employees at Safeco can trace their career path back to volunteerism experiences that taught them new skills, gave them confidence and earned them respect. But Mysliwy insists the company does not pressure employees to volunteer.

"We're talking about helping people grow, and that becomes the responsibility of the individual," he says. "We don't force people to do that. Work-life balance is important for us too. For some people, volunteering is an important part of their work-life balance. Others have responsibilities outside of work that preclude them from being able to spend time in volunteer activities."

"Volunteering should be just that," comments Dewey. "It should be optional. Mandatory volunteering is an oxymoron." Volunteer programs must be developed to mirror corporate culture and "done with sincerity, not merely for public relations benefits," he adds.

"It can't be forced," adds Remick, who suggests surveying employees to determine their interests before implementing a program.

Getting it right can yield tremendous rewards for a company, according to research on corporate philanthropy by The Council on Foundations and Walker Information. Employees who look favorably on their company's giving programs exhibit behaviors beneficial to business success and are many times more likely to remain with their employer, researchers found.

Steps to Ensure Success

To be successful, a volunteerism program must:

1. Acknowledge that employee volunteer efforts contribute to the achievement of business goals.

2. Focus workplace volunteering on specific social problems in the community that are identified with your business. Toy manufacturers might build playgrounds, for example.

3. Get senior management buy-in.

4. Determine time-off policies before implementing the program.

5. Promote collaboration across departments and divisions in developing the program.

6. Encourage the involvement of every employee.

7. Manage the program like any other business function.

Young People Are Volunteering in Unprecedented Numbers

Tania Deluzuriaga

Tania Deluzuriaga is a staff writer for the Orlando Sentinel.

Volunteerism is gaining currency among the youth of America, who need an outlet during their free time and a viable alternative to watching television and doing homework. Youngsters, who may have begun volunteering as a school requirement, often continue to volunteer of their own free will. When people begin volunteering at a young age, they often continue to do so as they grow older. At a time when many youths have voiced frustration with politics as an agent of change, volunteerism offers a practical way for them to truly make a difference in society.

They are young people with a sense of social responsibility and empowerment who are making their mark by solving problems, not causing them.

They are children such as Morgan Welch and Sarah Sheibenberger, a couple of Volusia County, Fla., 9-year-olds who wanted to help raise money for the DeBary Art League. The pair started the Can Do Cans Club and have raised about $500 collecting aluminum cans during the past nine months.

"It's fun helping people," said Morgan, who hit upon the idea after attending the art league's summer program. "I thought it was sad they didn't have their own building and I wanted to help them."

The New Generation Fix

Morgan and Sarah are just two of more than 72 million youths under age 25 in the nation, a group that is taking charge and addressing problems within their communities in numbers as never before. According to a study [2002] by the Center for Information & Research on Civic Learning & Engagement, 40 percent of people ages 15 to 25 reported volunteering in the past year, compared with 32 percent of Gen-Xers and 32 percent of baby boomers.

And that figure doesn't include preteens such as Morgan and Sarah, because most studies don't track the efforts of people that young even though elementary and middle school students are a big part of Generation Fix, said author Elizabeth Rusch, who coined the phrase in 2001 while interviewing youths ages 8 to 18 for her book of the same title.

"Society has this sense that we have to wait for kids to grow up," Rusch said. "But even young kids have the skills they need to be effective agents of change."

"Youth is the hope of today, not tomorrow," said Steve Culbertson, president of the Washington, D.C.-based Youth Service America, a resource center for youth-focused volunteer organizations. "They have incredible assets: energy, idealism and creativity."

Young people are pursuing long-lasting community change.

In Central Florida, Hands On Orlando boasts the largest National Youth Service Day contingent in the nation. More than 21,000 youths and adults volunteered [April 2003], participating in 151 projects that ranged from collecting food for the homeless to making cards for senior citizens to recording a CD of patriotic music for troops overseas.

"It's a great day, but it's only one day," said Chris Allen, director of Hands On Orlando.

"These types of projects are happening every day."

Empowering the Youth of America

The organization coordinates volunteer activities with hundreds of nonprofit groups throughout Central Florida. Participants simply go to the organization's Web site and sign up for a volunteer activity that interests them.

"We help kids understand community issues and the power they have to make a difference," Allen said.

These aren't just students who are cleaning up parks or volunteering because they have to, said Wendy Lesko, head of the Youth Activism Project in Washington, D.C., and author of the book "Youth!: The 26 Percent Solution."

"Young people are pursuing long-lasting community change," she said.

There is this animated and passionate generation of kids walking around with all sorts of ideas in their heads. . . . All it takes to get them out is a question.

Stacey Hillman, 12, saw a need for police dogs to have the same body protections as their human counterparts.

"I was reading an article about police dogs getting hurt in the line of duty and I thought about how I'd feel if something happened to my dog," she said.

Three years ago, she started Pennies to Protect Police Dogs, which has raised more than $200,000 to buy bulletproof vests for police dogs. The vests cost about $600 each. The Deltona seventh-grader has received national attention, and last year she was one of five middle-school students awarded the Prudential Community Spirit Award.

"I volunteer because I get to help out my community and try to make it better," she said.

The award comes with $25,000 worth of clothing and toys to be donated to a charity of her choice. Stacey donated the supplies to the Volusia and Osceola, Fla., sheriffs' offices.

Although schools and civic groups have long encouraged students to perform community service, youths today have taken volunteering to a new level, tackling social problems the way they once approached littered parks and canned food drives.

"There is this animated and passionate generation of kids walking around with all sorts of ideas in their heads," Rusch said. "All it takes to get them out is a question."

From a School Requirement to a Choice

The movement is starting in homes and in schools, experts said. Today, 96 percent of all school districts in the nation offer some type of community-service activity, up from 27 percent of districts in 1985, according to the National Service-Learning Clearinghouse, a national service-learning resource center in Scotts Valley, Calif. Nationwide, 18 percent of all school districts require students to do some community service, though many students also serve in order to be eligible for scholarships.

The requirements don't make students any less enthusiastic about the projects, Allen said. Rather, requirements are a good way to get students involved in their communities.

"Usually the volunteering starts out as a requirement," he said. "Once they get a taste, they see how they can make a difference and they want to stay involved."

A study last May [2002] found only 14 percent of students who volunteered said they did so because they had to. Most said they volunteered because someone else, such as a church or family member, asked them to help.

That was the case for 19-year-old Erica Jones. Besides being the youth spokesperson for Hands On Orlando, the University of Central Florida student is in the school's LEAD scholar program, which combines community service and leadership development classes. She started volunteering in middle school because her mother asked her to accompany her to homeless shelters and Habitat for Humanity projects.

I think that social consciousness has to be instilled early or they won't get it as an adult.

"It was getting out of bed that early in the morning that was the hard part," she said. "Once I got there, I always had a good time."

Jones continued volunteering in college, "because it doesn't feel like work. It feels like fun and you know you made a difference."

Starting Early Is Important

Youth service starts early and leads to greater involvement in the future; 66 percent of adults who volunteer now started volunteering as youths, according to a study by Independent Sector, a coalition in Washington, D.C., of more than 700 national nonprofit organizations.

That's why Phyllis Currie of Altamonte Springs, Fla., has encouraged and supported her daughter Nadine's community-service activities. "I think that social consciousness has to be instilled early or they won't get it as an adult," she said.

Though Nadine, 12, accompanies her mother to service projects, she also plans her own. In 2001, she launched a letter-writing campaign on behalf of the St. Johns River Water Management District's aquatic plant rehabilitation project in Lake Apopka, Fla. Her letter persuaded the Sara Lee Corp. to donate 6,000 pairs of athletic socks to the project. The socks were filled with sand and used to anchor bulrush plants to the lake bottom. Nadine got the Governor's Points of Light Award for her efforts.

More recently, the Teague Middle School in Altamonte Springs, Fla., sixth-grader organized a landscaping project at her school for National Youth Service Day. The project focused on integrating native and drought-resistant plants to the school's landscape.

"In our society, watching TV and doing homework isn't enough," Nadine said. "Kids need something else to do."

For most, involvement begins at a grass-roots level with students identifying problems in their communities and finding creative ways to solve them. "Grass roots engages kids at a level where they want to be engaged," Allen said. "It's so much more direct, they really can see the difference they're making."

Volunteerism as an Alternative to Voting

However, although volunteering has increased during the past 20 years, voter turnout for people age 18 to 24 has dropped 15 percentage points, according to the Center for Information & Research on Civic Learning & Engagement.

Service has become the politics of Generation Fix, Culbertson said. "Many young people see service as an alternative to voting because they're disgusted with the system," he said. "They think their vote has no impact, where service does. There's no question that there's a danger to that."

Getting youths to see the connection between community participation and public policy will be key to increasing political participation among young people, he said. Once that happens, Culbertson predicts political reformation that's sensitive to big-money interests and cares about fairness, equality and doing the right thing.

"We're going to see a generation of politicians that will turn the politics as we know it upside-down," he said.

8

Mandatory Volunteerism for Students Is a Farce

Carlos Ramos-Mrosovsky

Carlos Ramos-Mrosovsky wrote this article as a senior at Princeton University, where he founded the journal American Foreign Policy.

When high school students must perform community service in order to impress college admissions officers, too often their service is more self-serving than beneficial to the community. Nevertheless, mandatory service has become a requirement for admission to prestigious colleges. This forced service has created numerous dilemmas. Students who want to impress colleges with their leadership skills may create charitable foundations that are impractical and do little to help the community. Worse still, some students have documented falsified or exaggerated community service on their college applications. Community service should not be enforced by high schools or colleges. If this occurs, community service will become just another mandatory school requirement.

"So," I asked, "what are you doing this summer?" "I'm setting up a nonprofit to help at-risk youth attend college."

"That's great," I replied. "How are you going to fund it?" Pause. "That's kind of the problem. I don't really know how to get any money for it."

I was speaking with a certified "young leader" of the sort one meets at student leadership conferences. He knew very well that it would be extremely difficult to get a new nonprofit started, and that he could accomplish much more at a preexisting charity. But he went ahead anyway.

This kind of conversation is very common among undergraduates and college-bound high-school seniors. Set against calls from prominent figures on both left and right to make "community service" a nationwide requirement for graduation from high school, stories like this should give us pause.

The Dark Side of Student Volunteerism

It is one thing for society to appreciate community service, but quite another to require it. Where it is already in place, mandatory service often contributes to a culture of hypocrisy. It can undermine young people's respect for and interest in genuine *volunteerism*. To understand this darker side of student *volunteerism* one need look no further than the admissions office at any major university.

Says one classmate of mine: 'I stopped doing community service after my high school forced me into it. It wasn't generous. I did it for me, not for anyone else.'

Students get into top colleges through hard work and by learning the tacit rules of the admissions game. Genius is rarely the secret of entry. Admissions officers demand not only perfect grades but also prodigious extracurricular or athletic achievements, and community service. Insiders like to call this mix "the triple S," for "scholarship, sports, and service." In other words, if you haven't done enough hours collecting dimes to save the whales from hungry Icelanders, then you had best play the cello like Yo-Yo Ma, and be a mean lineman to boot.

It's good for the best and brightest to feel a call to serve the community. But from this student's perspective, making service into a virtual entry requirement is a moral trap: What universities look for as a sign of selflessness, students undertake as a way to get into college and get their careers started. Benefit to the community can become merely incidental. This corrosive paradox makes many students cynical about community service. Says one classmate of mine: "I stopped doing community service after my high school forced me into it. It wasn't generous. I did it for me, not for anyone else." Many more would probably admit the same sentiments, at least after a few beers.

Students Serve Themselves More Than They Serve Others

Just how self-serving can college-bound community service get? Consider this headline from www.StudentNow.com, a website that offers advice to prospective scholars: "Be a Triple Threat: Combine Academics, Activities and Community Service." Community service "used to be a big plus" advises www.CollegeConfidential.com. "Now, however, it's almost the norm, especially at the more competitive colleges." This advice reflects a confusion on the part of college admissions offices: In their zeal to recruit Samaritans, colleges have attracted a great number of Pharisees [hypocrites].

For many, these pressures continue on to higher levels of the admissions and resume sweepstakes. Students interested in graduate schools, professional schools, and prestigious fellowships and scholarships are also advised to document their do-gooding. Sometimes the distortion of priorities diminishes the benefit to those one purports to help, as can be seen in the conversation at the start of this article.

The fact is that, with a few laudable exceptions, most of the volunteer work performed by college students is too small-scale and fragmentary to improve the world much. One Princeton student's experiences building a school on a summer service trip to Ghana illustrate this well. "Before I went to Ghana, I didn't realize how ineffective it would be. The school hasn't bettered their lives," he says. "I'm a lot less interested in micro-volunteering." Many students who volunteer in American inner cities report similar feelings.

It seems like no good deed can go uncatalogued, if you want to get ahead.

What's more, colleges place a premium on leadership as well as service. This means that applicants tend to fare better when they start their own charitable projects, rather than join preexisting ones. Often, the limited time and resources available to high-school students translate into less valuable achievements but better-sounding resume items. For example, one might found an organization to collect prom dresses for the homeless rather than work at a soup kitchen run by a local church.

Forced Volunteerism Leads to Fakery

Outright fakery comes a few steps beyond distorted motivations. In a recent case, a Harvard-bound New Jersey kid—who made national news by taking her school to court to be made sole valedictorian—was caught plagiarizing columns she wrote for a local newspaper. Moreover, according to the *Philadelphia Inquirer*, her father aided her extensive community-service projects, delivering food to food banks and otherwise doing much of the work. The girl, who was also admitted to Princeton, Duke, Stanford, and Cornell, ultimately had her admission to Harvard revoked because of the plagiarism.

These examples are remarkable only in their degree. Ask students at Princeton or comparable institutions about their experiences applying to college in high school. Chances are they'll tell you a story about the student whose parents set up a charitable trust in her name, or the girl who boldly raised awareness of the dangers of littering while her parents smothered the local paper with press releases. Little wonder that many students are skeptical of classmates' service projects and especially those that aim to raise "awareness," which they see as easiest to set up and get credit for.

Some of the most genuinely service-oriented students refuse to accept credit for their good deeds. Rejecting a culture of hypocrisy, one college junior in Massachusetts omits her hours of work at a school for autistic children from her resume. But, she says, despairingly, "I don't know if I can sustain that"—she plans to apply to graduate school. "It seems like no good deed can go uncatalogued, if you want to get ahead." Ironically, the forces that give rise to careerist community service can actually obscure the genuine article.

Mandatory Service
May Be No Service at All

Yet despite its ambiguous effects on college students, mandatory volunteer work is increasingly popular with politicians and school boards across the country. High schools from Los Angeles to Washington, D.C., have already imposed quotas of a given number of hours of service students must perform. With these come all the easily predicted problems—unfairness to poorer students who need free time to work (for money), the problem of defining what fulfills the requirement (faith-based charities anyone?), inefficiency, and politicization.

Made mandatory by law, rather than by competitive pressures, the problem would worsen. If students can already view service as something that you do if you want to get ahead, imagine how they will regard service were it to become something you have to do just to graduate. Advocates of a national community-service requirement understandably want to inculcate the values of good citizenship and community in youth. They should reflect that the value they are trying to promote depends on a sense of duty, not necessity. They risk exacerbating a dynamic through which students may increasingly come to see volunteer service as just one more box to check on the climb of life: the moral equivalent of gym class, sex education, or chemistry.

And that would be no service at all.

9

Mandatory Student Volunteerism Benefits Everyone Involved

Melissa M. Ezarik

Melissa M. Ezarik is a Connecticut-based freelance writer.

Many public schools, including all of those in Maryland, require students to perform public service in order to graduate; however, what starts as a forced school requirement can lead to a lifelong passion for the volunteer. Students who volunteer find their own self-esteem rises as they become valuable members of the community. Their service to others often leads them to develop important life skills such as teamwork and leadership. Volunteering can also lead a young person toward a career goal. But the best reward of all is the way in which volunteers help others to lead more enjoyable lives.

When Rachel Doyle's grandmother passed away in 1999 in a Nevada nursing home, it was because of loneliness and refusing to eat. The next year, as a junior in high school, Rachel founded a nonprofit organization in hopes of preventing the same thing from happening to other grandmothers.

Called GlamourGals, the New York-based organization pairs teens with female residents in nursing homes. After the teens collect donations of facial cleansers, cosmetics, and instant camera film, they meet at the home to perform makeovers on the residents.

"The women love it! They smile and tell life stories about when they were our age and their experiences with makeup," says Rachel, now 20, and a junior at Cornell University. "After the makeover, the women smile for the camera—some of them pose like 1930s starlets. They are so cute!"

The elderly women feel a renewed sense of their own beauty. But they're not the only ones to benefit. "Many think that volunteering is all about what you give. But what catches you by surprise is how much you receive in return," Rachel says.

Everyone Benefits From Mandatory Public Service

Within the past 10 years, more and more teens have stepped up as volunteers, some because their schools require students to perform service work.

For example, Maryland requires 75 hours of student service for graduation. But what started as a school assignment for three friends at Montgomery Blair High School in Silver Spring, Maryland, has become their passion. Then-sophomores Matthew Yalowitz, Sarah Thibadeau, and Annie Pierce created the Montgomery Ultimate Story Exchange (MUSE) three years ago.

Elementary students are invited to join an after-school club where they're matched up with a high school mentor. Each week, the young students send their creative writing to the mentors via E-mail. The mentors respond with compliments and suggestions on the writing. "That E-mail can make a huge impact on the students," says Matt, now 18. One student from Liberia [in Africa], for example, was a shy, hesitant writer at first. With his mentor's encouragement, he eventually wrote about his family and life in Liberia. From then on, the boy opened up.

Everyone benefits. The kids learn that writing and technology can be fun, and the high school students become proud role models. The program now has 40 mentors. Over time, the founders of MUSE have watched their dream become reality.

Volunteering Makes One Feel Good

Luke Fritsch also volunteers with youngsters. As a T-ball coach for the past two years, the 18-year-old says he enjoys it when the kids spot him around town. Hearing an enthusiastic "Hi, Coach!" or getting a compliment from a parent, he says, "really makes my day."

Samuel Richard Prunty, a freshman at the University of Wisconsin in Madison, has made a difference in the lives of people he's never even met. His parents helped start a fund to raise money for projects in East Africa. "Many of the projects we help fund are for children. I know that I have touched them, by the letters and [by] seeing their happy faces in the pictures we receive," he says. "It makes it worth the time and effort."

Volunteerism Promotes Skill Building

As a bonus, volunteering can help you build skills that are useful in school and in the workplace too. Here are some of the skills participants often develop.

Organizational skills. Rachel learned that founding a program takes lots of planning. Before the first GlamourGals makeover was held, Rachel spent months writing grant applications, soliciting donations, raising money, recruiting volunteers, and learning how nonprofits work. The first event went smoothly because of her careful coordination.

Communication skills. The MUSE founders found themselves speaking in front of the state legislature when it considered dropping the service work requirement for schools. How well did they communicate the reasons it should remain in place? "The bill was defeated," Matt says. In his future career in political science or international relations, that public speaking practice will definitely come in handy.

Luke's coaching taught him how to communicate with kids. "I have learned to make things concise and interesting to hold their attention," he says.

Samuel's volunteer work has taught him to deal with all kinds of people. This has paid off at his job at the local library. "If you're nice and helpful, it makes someone's day a lot better," he says.

Whether starting a program from scratch or taking on a leadership position at an organization, volunteering can mean learning to take charge.

Even one of the first steps toward volunteering—finding a good organization—can boost your ability to communicate clearly. Great Givers, a program that helps teens get into volunteering, suggests asking an organization you're interested in a few questions before you sign up. Some important ones are: What exactly would I be doing as a volunteer? What results has the program achieved? What percentage of donations actually go to the program?

Teamwork. Samuel has learned that a volunteering event is most successful when everyone pitches in. He remembers this lesson whenever it's time to buckle down and get a group project completed at school.

Rachel says she feels a sense of teamwork, not only among the caring people who work for GlamourGals, but also from her supportive family. "I could not have done it alone," she says.

Leadership. Whether starting a program from scratch or taking on a leadership position at an organization, volunteering can mean learning to take charge. Rachel has watched GlamourGals grow from one chapter to 10. She speaks at youth conferences, encouraging other teens to do fundraising and take on leadership roles in organizations. Her work has even been featured in a number of national publications and television shows. "It is almost surreal how much the program has grown, and the success it has achieved," she says.

Volunteers Make a Real Difference

Volunteering now can help you get a jump on your career goals. "Knowing that I wanted to become a teacher, I have actively searched for opportunities to interact with kids," says Luke, a freshman at the University of Wisconsin, Eau Claire. "The thrill that you get out of helping younger generations grow and become better people," he adds, is what continues to draw him to the profession.

While volunteering didn't influence Samuel's main career choice, he says that learning how rewarding it was to serve others did help him make another choice. In college, he'll be studying to be an electrical engineer, but at the same time, he'll be serving his country as an Air Force R.O.T.C. member.

Of course, among the best things about volunteering are the personal rewards. Once, Rachel was giving a makeover to a woman who didn't seem to be enjoying it. "I kept up the energy, smiling and laughing," Rachel says, remembering how disappointed she felt that her efforts didn't seem to be working.

A few days later, the nursing home activities director called to explain that the woman had been severely depressed and had not been eating for a while. After the makeover, she had started eating again. That's when Rachel knew for sure that her program was making a real difference.

10

Volunteers for Medical Research Are Desperately Needed

Virginia A. Smith

Virginia A. Smith is a staff writer for the Philadelphia Inquirer.

Clinical trials, in which pharmaceutical companies and medical professionals study the effect of new treatments and drugs on volunteer patients, are critical to the development of cures for diseases. However, recruiting volunteers for these studies has proven extremely difficult. Potential volunteers are often scared off by stories of patient abuse, fear of being given a placebo instead of the actual medicine, or the possibility of long and complex procedures. Moreover, many volunteers who begin clinical trials drop out before the end. In order to attract and retain volunteers, pharmaceutical companies need to do a better job of educating the public about the benefits of clinical trials. It has been especially difficult to recruit women, who are busy with family responsibilities, and African Americans who are leery of government-sponsored medical studies because of past abuses; however, those who do participate may see their health improve as a result.

The medical world needs more Phyllis Morellos.

This self-effacing nursery-school teacher from Garfield, N.J., volunteered for one of the hundreds of clinical trials in the Philadelphia region, agreeing to have an experimental

Virginia A. Smith, "Volunteers Hard to Find for Clinical Trials," *Knight Ridder Newspapers*, April 16, 2004. Copyright © 2004 *Knight Ridder Newspapers*. Reproduced by permission.

pacemaker implanted in her stomach to see if it would help her digestive problems.

Although millions of other sick people are enrolled in clinical trials to test new treatments, the number falls far short of the growing demands of corporations and medical centers that compete in a mad, expensive dash to market new products.

Hard as it is to attract patient volunteers, it's even harder to keep them.

Three million Americans do manage to complete clinical trials each year, put so many others drop out that 90 percent of trials never make it to the end, according to Thomson CenterWatch, a Boston nonprofit that tracks the clinical trials industry.

"You can't bring drugs through the pipeline if you can't adequately test them, and the patient recruitment problem has slowed the pipeline to a crawl," said Dan McDonald, CenterWatch vice president.

There are many possible explanations.

Patients may not know enough about clinical trials. They may be scared off by the risks, or by revelations of deaths or abuses. They may fear being given a placebo. They may be too busy.

And then there are the trials themselves—bigger, longer and more complex, requiring more patients than ever.

The Business of Recruiting Volunteers

"Patient recruitment is the No. 1 roadblock to getting drug trials done," said Kathleen Drennan, of Iris Global Clinical Trial Solutions in Chicago.

In true American fashion, the problem has spawned a new growth industry: private companies such as Drennan's that recruit and retain volunteers, a growing number of whom now come from India, Eastern Europe and South America, where patients are often desperate for treatment.

It's a scramble with a potentially grand payoff. The drug giants' future earnings depend on finding the next breakthrough treatment or blockbuster drug, which in turn can mean life or death for sick people.

"People have to realize this is serious business," said John I. Gallin, director of the National Institutes of Health [NIH] Clinical center in Bethesda, Md., where 1,100 clinical trials are going on. "This is what's going to move us forward in developing better care and prevention of disease."

Clinical trials test potential new drugs, devices or procedures in patient volunteers over time to see if they meet standards for general use. Some volunteers are paid.

More than 70,000 trials are conducted annually in this country alone, funded by about $6 billion a year from private drug and biotech companies and the NIH. They are carried out by research institutes, medical schools, hospitals and private trial-management firms, and overseen by local review boards and the U.S. Food and Drug Administration [FDA].

Some trials easily attract volunteers, said Ken Getz, founder of CenterWatch and chairman of the Center for Information and Study on Clinical Research Participation in Boston. He cited male pattern baldness and other so-called vanity illnesses.

Morello had never heard of clinical trials but figured if this one failed, she was no worse off. 'If you're sick, you have nothing to lose,' she said.

But everyone else in the industry, he said, "is having a terrible time. It's the biggest problem today."

And the need for patients doesn't go away after a drug wins FDA approval.

GlaxoSmithKline, London-based with U.S. headquarters in Philadelphia and North Carolina, will be investing $300 million in long-term studies of Avandia, a drug for Type II diabetes that won FDA approval in 1999. "You have to look at it for years and years, even after the drug is approved," said company spokesman Rick Koenig.

Getting one new drug tested and approved, drugmakers estimate, takes seven years and costs $897 million, a figure "Big Pharma" critics say is inflated to justify high drug prices.

Benefits and Risks of Volunteering

Whatever the true cost, none of this can happen without patients like Morello, 46, who was despondent when she arrived at Temple University School of Medicine two years ago.

For years, she had suffered from gastroparesis, a common disorder that prevents even small amounts of water from being digested. She was throwing up 24 times a day. "It was depressing," she said.

Morello had never heard of clinical trials but figured if this one failed, she was no worse off. "If you're sick, you have nothing to lose," she said.

One in 30 patient volunteers experiences a serious side effect and one in 10,000 dies . . .

Things slowly began to improve. "I could sit in the car or go to the mall and have a bottle of water with me," she said. "It's just a normal thing for everyone else, but I was ecstatic."

Aaron Shostack, 43, of Pottstown, Pa., hasn't been so lucky. Shostack, who is HIV positive, has volunteered for several Philadelphia drug trials since 1990. None helped, but he remains committed to volunteering. "When you have an illness and there's no real light at the end of the tunnel," he said, "the way I look at it, anything I can do, I'm willing to do."

The biggest recruiting problem, many believe, is that patients haven't heard of clinical trials and don't know that a commitment might last only eight to 18 months. "Industry and the medical profession have done a pretty lousy job of educating the public about clinical trials," said Drennan.

And bad news travels fast: One in 30 patient volunteers experiences a serious side effect and one in 10,000 dies, according to CenterWatch.

Sometimes, patients are just too busy.

"The patient may say, 'I'm from New York' or 'There's a traffic jam' or 'I work' or 'Can I come see you on Saturday?'" said Henry P. Parkman, the Temple gastroenterologist who runs Morello's trial, one of 101 at the medical school.

Sometimes it's the primary-care physicians who are too busy to refer patients to trials.

Women and African American Volunteers Are Scarce

Women are hard to recruit, investigators say, because of family responsibilities. The underrepresentation of blacks in studies is often blamed on the legacy of the government-sponsored Tuskegee syphilis study in the mid-1900s. Four hundred black Alabama sharecroppers received no treatment for syphilis so the disease could be studied.

"Tuskegee . . . is still an important part of the African-American relationship with the health-care establishment," said Vanessa Northington Gamble, a medical historian and physician at Johns Hopkins School of Public Health in Baltimore.

She cautioned, however, that the black community's distrust of medical trials did not begin—or end—with Tuskegee.

Jane Shull, executive director of Philadelphia FIGHT, said her AIDS service organization has enrolled hundreds of minority patients in clinical trials. She suggested that "provider behavior" is the problem. "It's prejudice," she said. "They believe people of color either won't understand the study or will be unreliable. The truth is, they just don't try to sign them up."

CenterWatch estimates that $500 million will be spent this year on advertising to recruit patients. And everywhere the talk is about educating the public and making the trial experience more customer-friendly.

Meanwhile, Morello may never be able to handle a Thanksgiving feast, but she eats salads and raw vegetables and occasionally goes out for dinner.

She now throws up "only" four or five times a day. "Everybody has something," she said cheerfully. "This is what I have to deal with."

11

Researchers Must Be Honest with Clinical Trial Volunteers

Avery Hurt

Avery Hurt is a contributing editor to New Physician. *He also writes for* Better Homes and Gardens, Newsweek, *and* Life Health.

Clinical trials are a necessity when it comes to medical research, and attracting enough volunteers to conduct experiments is essential. Despite the gains to be made in medical research, there are inherent dangers in subjecting volunteers to such experimentation. Volunteers have died during what they thought were essentially harmless clinical trials. Two practical issues have made it more difficult to ensure the safety of modern clinical trials: first, private industry does the majority of clinical trials (in the past, government agencies did most of the research) and these trials must be cost effective; second, there are so many trials currently being conducted that institutional review boards (IRBs), which monitor the trials, are completely overworked. Researchers run a fine line between keeping volunteers completely informed about the potentially dangerous nature of the experiments and still being able to attract volunteers. No matter the cost to research, it is essential that subjects be clearly informed about the nature of the experiments for which they are volunteering.

In 1796 Dr. Edward Jenner began what may have been the first clinical trial in the history of medicine. In order to test his theory about a vaccination for smallpox, the physician infected an 8-year-old volunteer, a boy named James Phipps, with live cowpox virus. Seven weeks later, he infected the child with live smallpox virus. As Jenner suspected, the milder cowpox virus provided the boy with immunity to the much more serious smallpox virus. After this triumph, Jenner conducted more tests on volunteers. His experiments were astoundingly successful, eventually leading to a vaccination for smallpox that all but eliminated a disease that had previously ravaged Europe and Asia, killing and disfiguring millions of people.

Looking at Jenner's research from a 21st-century perspective, most modern scientists would agree that his method's results and the risks he took to get them are impressive. We will never know what agonies of conscience Jenner suffered as he considered the potential dangers and benefits of testing his theory. But we do know that the dilemma he faced is one that all clinical researchers face in one way or another. Even in today's much more controlled medical environments, experiments on humans are not without risks. The potential good for the individuals who participate in clinical trials must be carefully balanced against the possible risks to a few volunteers. Dealing with these dilemmas is not made any easier by the current climate of biomedical research. An overworked oversight system, complex financial arrangements, and ever more complex and intractable diseases make the challenging job of a clinical researcher even more difficult.

The Dangers of Volunteering for Clinical Trials

Ellen Roche was not sick when she enrolled in a study at Johns Hopkins Asthma and Allergy Center last year [2001]. A month after her enrollment, however, she was dead. The experiment in which she participated was designed to examine how healthy lungs keep airways open even when they are exposed to irritating substances. No new drugs or therapies were being tested in this trial. The drug Roche was given and that likely led to her death—hexamethonium bromide, a lung irritant—had been prescribed decades ago to treat hypertension and to reduce bleeding during surgery. Yet it was never approved by the Food and Drug Administration (FDA) to be inhaled, which was how Roche's clinical trial was administering it, and it isn't currently approved by the FDA for use in humans at all.

No one knows why Roche, a healthy, 24-year-old lab technician, volunteered for what was supposed to be a low-risk experiment. It may have been simple curiosity, an altruistic desire to advance science and help others, or perhaps she needed the $365 she would have received if she had completed the study. Roche was not, however, desperate for a cure for asthma (she did not have the disorder), and in any case, she understood that the medication she received was not a therapy and that she would gain no health benefits by participating in the trial. . . .

The lab technician's death is not the only incident in recent years to raise questions about safety procedures in clinical trials. Since 1998, concerns about the safety of human research subjects have halted hundreds of experiments. Perhaps the most disturbing case, as well as the most publicized, was in 1999—the death of Jesse Gelsinger, an 18-year-old volunteer in a gene therapy trial at the University of Pennsylvania.

Like Roche, Gelsinger was not sick when he entered the trial. He did, however, suffer from a rare genetic disorder, ornithine transcarbamylase (OTC) deficiency. The disease affects the body's ability to break down ammonia and is almost always fatal; most children who are born with OTC deficiency die within their first year, and survival beyond the age of 5 is extremely rare. Gelsinger suffered from a milder form of the deficiency, and medication and a strict diet kept his condition under control. The trial was designed to help develop a therapy for babies with the disease. Ethicists had determined that parents of babies with OTC deficiency could not give truly informed consent for their children to participate in the study, since they may be unduly influenced by their children's illness. Instead it was decided the experiment would be done on mothers who were carriers of the disease and adult males, like Gelsinger, who had a milder form of OTC deficiency.

The experiment entailed some risks, but Gelsinger was aware of this. He said that he was doing it for "the babies." The teenager died of multiple organ failure after being injected with adenovirus vectors designed to replace the faulty genetic information with the proper instructions.

Gelsinger's death, the first reported death in a gene therapy trial, was a tremendous blow not only, of course, to his family and friends, but also to gene therapy research. After his death, the University of Pennsylvania was forced to halt all genetic research involving human subjects—a major setback for the institution that leads the nation in genetic research.

A Flawed System

The deaths of Roche and Gelsinger, as well as other recent clinical trials cases involving violations or errors, have provoked intense scrutiny of the U.S. clinical trials system and the procedures designed to ensure the safety of human research primarily those involving the OHRP [Office of Human Research Protections] and IRBs [institutional review boards].

Dr. Greg Koski, the OHRP's director since September 2000, calls the current clinical trials system "dysfunctional." Other experts agree, saying the current system is in dire need of improvement, if not a total overhaul. Financial conflicts of interest, lack of full disclosure about the details of previous studies, and consent forms that are difficult to understand have all been cited as significant flaws.

For example, while Gelsinger knew that his participation in the study entailed some risk, he did not know the gene therapy he received had resulted in the deaths of some primates during the animal phase of the study. Nor did he know the study's chief investigator owned stock in the company funding the research.

Concerns in relation to funding sources are common. In the past, government agencies sponsored the majority of medical research. Today, pharmaceutical companies and other private industries and foundations fund more than half of the research that is being conducted in the United States. Critics of the system say this can easily lead to conflicts of interest as well as restrictions on how information is shared among researchers within the academic community. The National Institutes of Health has expressed grave concern about the ability of private enterprise to protect academic freedom in scientific research, and to determine and enforce appropriate limits of financial interests.

Another major problem is the IRB system. IRBs are designed to scrutinize and approve every piece of proposed research that will involve human subjects. However, the recent explosion of biomedical research—an estimated 5,000 institutions conduct clinical trials—has resulted in IRBs that are so overworked that doing their jobs well is almost impossible.

"When Ellen Roche died, 2,500 studies were under review by the various review boards at Hopkins," says Alan Milstein, an attorney who has filed numerous lawsuits on behalf of clinical trials volunteers, including representing Gelsinger's father in his case against the University of Pennsylvania, which settled out of court. "At any given time, between 200,000 and 300,000 studies are being done that involve human subjects. With this much research going on, the oversight system simply can't do what it is mandated to do," he says.

Dr. John Zaia, chair of the IRB at City of Hope Cancer Center in Los Angeles, agrees. "IRBs are totally snowed under. The biggest problem is that IRBs don't have the staffing to deal with the increased workload," he says.

Reform Is Difficult

But even when the problems can be identified, correcting them is not easy. The biomedical research community is a huge conglomeration of academic medical centers, private research labs, government agencies and private foundations. Enforcement authority and regulations vary from institution to institution, and protocols and reporting guidelines often change depending on who is funding the research.

For example, in 1981, the HHS [U.S. Department of Health and Human Services] established a set of regulations that have since developed into what is now known as the Common Rule. These regulations are designed to oversee the protection of human research subjects and to detail the responsibilities of oversight committees such as IRBs. However, the rule applies only to federally funded research and any changes to its provisions must be approved by as many as 17 federal agencies.

"When the [oversight] system gets too cumbersome, it stops functioning as a protective mechanism for either the researcher or the patients," says Dr. Carla Falkson, a cancer researcher at the University of Alabama at Birmingham's (UAB) Comprehensive Cancer Center.

Much of the problem with the system stems from volunteers' unrealistic expectations of the biomedical process . . .

The OHRP's Koski has repeatedly stressed the need for open and honest cooperation between institutions (researchers, universities and their IRBs) and the government oversight offices. Under his watch, he says, the OHRP has been willing to use its authority to enforce regulations, but it can't reform the system on its own. Institutions need to improve research protections voluntarily, he says. Some institutions are doing this. After the deaths of Roche and Gelsinger, Hopkins and the University of Pennsylvania have increased the number of IRBs and changed the practices of the boards so they can more closely monitor the research. . . .

Volunteers Often Don't Understand What They Are Volunteering For

Like many ethics experts, Rebecca Dresser believes there are serious flaws in the clinical trials system but points to another area of grave concern—communication. Much of the problem with the system stems from volunteers' unrealistic expectations of the biomedical process, says the professor of biomedical ethics at Washington University School of Law and author of *When Science Offers Salvation: Patient Advocacy and Research Ethics.*

"Researchers haven't done a very good job of informed consent," Dresser says. "People already have an impression when they walk into the researcher's office—usually a positive impression—about the research. This may lead patients to not pay as much attention as they should to what the researcher is telling them about the trial."

Volunteers aren't the only ones at fault, though. "Researchers sometimes have an understandable reluctance to be brutally honest with people who are dying, who may be desperate for a cure," she says. "This lack of brutal honesty may mean that some people who are used in trials don't fully understand the chance of benefit."

Ethicists call this "therapeutic misconception," and researchers, when they acknowledge it at all, soon realize that it is the thorniest of issues they face when trying to justify the use of human subjects in medical experiments.

The fact is that most trials—especially phase one and phase two trials—offer participants very little chance of therapeutic benefit. Yet, few participants in clinical trials are doing it "for the babies"; most desperately seek a cure. Falkson describes the patients who volunteer for her studies as "people who've tried everything but don't want to give up hope. They know there is only a 1 to 2 percent chance of a response [to the experimental therapy], but they are willing to take that chance."

If patients truly understood the benefits and risks, fewer people would volunteer for experiments.

When asked if she is confident that her patients understand the possible risks and benefits of the experiment, Falkson nods sincerely. But she adds that "sometimes people don't want to know. We mustn't overestimate the ability of patients to comprehend the situation. Sometimes they are too emotionally involved with this to be rational. We have to handle them very gently."

Medicine Versus Science

The therapeutic misconception arises when patients, and often the physicians who recommend them for trials, confuse "medicine" and "science." In medicine, the goal is to alleviate suffering, perhaps to heal. In science, the goal is to advance knowledge with the prospect of eventually giving medicine better tools with which to pursue its goals. The role of patients in the clinical trials process is to volunteer their bodies to help researchers test theories so the scientific community can increase its knowledge. The role of researchers is, in part, to ensure the volunteers understand this. This is not an easy task, and this is why therapeutic misconception can be such a problem.

As Falkson pointed out, many volunteers are willing to try anything—to take any number of unknown risks for a minimal chance that this new therapy will cure their diseases or at least buy them more time. But here's the dilemma: If human research subjects were not so desperate, and if they truly understood the odds, would they still volunteer? Probably not, Milstein says.

"If patients truly understood the benefits and risks, fewer people would volunteer for experiments. People volunteer because they think it is in their therapeutic best interest. No matter what the researcher says, the patient will believe that the 'doctor' has the patient's best interest at heart. You don't find a lot of altruists in cancer wards and children's hospitals," Milstein says.

Dresser agrees there's a great disconnection between the research community and the average patient. "Our expectations for biomedical research are probably too great," she says. "Research definitely provides benefits, but if you spend time around medical schools, you soon realize that medical research is a slow and incremental process. There are many dead ends."

But despite the risky nature of the beast, if cures are to be found and advances are to be made, experiments have to be done, and human subjects are, at least at some point in the process, essential. Dr. David Curiel, director of UAB's Gene Therapy Center, is adamant on this point. One of the reasons he came to UAB to conduct his cutting-edge genetic research is because the university has an effective "bench-to-bedside" program.

"A strong linkage between the basic scientists and the clinic scientists is ideal," he says. "We design something in the lab, and then we are able to put it into a trial right here. We get answers in the clinic that tell us what we need to do to fix the problems in the lab." And that's the crux of the issue, he says. Human subjects are needed to fix, adjust and refine the science long before the science is ready to cure anyone.

Researchers Must Be Honest With Volunteers

So, back to that old ethical dilemma: Saving untold millions of people from the horrors of smallpox required risking the lives of healthy volunteers. Did Jenner's volunteers understand the nature of the risk? Perhaps. Was it worth it? It certainly seems so now. But these questions come up again and again, every day, in academic medical centers. And they aren't any easier to answer now than they were 200 years ago. But one thing, critics say, is certain: A responsible approach to medicine, whether in treating patients or recruiting them for studies, requires being as honest as possible with patients, even when they don't want to know or don't want to understand.

"If honesty with subjects means that the pace of research is slowed, then that is the price we pay for truth," Milstein says. "There are more important values than research, such as treating people as autonomous human beings and not as means to an end, putting their immediate safety and needs ahead of other, less tangible, concerns."

This is not a new idea. It is, in fact, one of the concepts on which the practice of medicine was founded: *primum non nocere*. First do no harm.

12

The Minutemen Volunteers Are True Patriots

Robert Klein Engler

Robert Klein Engler is an adjunct professor at Roosevelt University in Chicago, and has written op-ed articles, poetry, and philosophy. He is the author of the book A Winter of Words.

The volunteers of the minuteman project are caught between opposing political forces in the battle over illegal immigration. On one side is big business, which requires cheap labor and is concerned only with profits. On the other side are supporters of an open border policy, who favor globalism and who do not respect U.S. sovereignty. Both these camps see illegal immigrants as abstractions, and therefore do not feel the necessity to deal with the immigrants as human beings who are breaking U.S. laws. The minutemen volunteers are among the few in the United States who see the problem for what it is and want to do something about it. They recognize that illegal immigrants are political pawns in a larger battle, and seek a practical way to protect the United States.

The border between the United States and Mexico is flat and desolate along much of its 2,000 mile stretch. There is hardly any place high enough to get above the terrain where you may look down and see the larger picture that makes up the panorama of illegal immigration.

At points along the United States/Mexican border, members of the Minuteman Project keep watch. They ask that our

Robert Klein Engler, "Why the Minuteman Project Is Important," AmericanDaily.com, June 23, 2006. Reproduced by permission of the author.

immigration laws be enforced and want to inform the public about the harm illegal immigration does to our nation. They are not vigilantes, but they are vigilant.

Minuteman Volunteers are Caught Between Opposing Forces

Caught between the forces of big business on the one hand, and the open border lobby on the other hand, members of the Minuteman Project are among the few who rise above the desolate terrain of the border and see the truth about illegal immigration. This earns them the disdain of both the political right and left.

The open border lobby and their one world supporters take a Marxist view of illegal immigration. Those who want a world without borders see illegal immigrants as simply workers. They see illegal immigrants as pawns in a struggle towards a global, socialist revolution.

Is it little wonder that those who want open borders always talk about how hard illegal immigrants work, or how all they want is to support their families? For these open border lobbyists, illegal immigrants are not human beings fleeing a corrupt country, but workers who have a life only because they fulfill a function in a discredited theory of revolution.

The open border protesters we saw marching [on] May Day [of 2005] also want to diminish the power and sovereignty of the United States. In the final analysis, they would like to get rid of the United States as a nation. The old slogan of "workers of the WORLD, unite!" [the rallying cry of socialism] still echoes in their heart since it was proposed more than 150 years ago.

The proponents of big business aren't much different from the socialists when it comes to illegal immigration. All they see are abstract workers, too, when they look at illegal immigrants pouring into the United States from Mexico. The managers of international corporations care more about profits than they do about citizenship and patriotism, so it makes no difference to them where their workers originate.

[M]embers of the Minuteman Project are important because they have a realistic view of illegal immigration.

It makes no difference to transnational elites if a worker is in the United States legally or illegally, either. Patriotism and citizenship are irrelevant to the international flow of capital. Patriotism and citizenship may even be an obstacle to increased profits by placing limits on exploitation.

The elites in big business would have the borders open. Then, workers could move as freely as digital bank accounts. If not that, then the elites would have a guest worker program that masks an amnesty. For the elites of big business, illegal immigrants are not persons, but cogs in a great industrial and agricultural machine.

Minuteman Volunteers View Illegal Immigration Realistically

Caught in the middle between two abstractions, the proponents of open borders and the elites of big business, members of the Minuteman Project are important because they have a realistic view of illegal immigration. Members of the Minuteman Project do not look upon illegal immigrants from Mexico and elsewhere as abstract workers who are pawns in the struggle between socialists and capitalist.

Instead, members of the Minuteman Project see that from both sides of the border, the issue of illegal immigration involves human beings and not just abstractions. From the Minuteman Project's point of view, what is ultimately at stake in the debate over illegal immigration is the very human question of citizenship and identity.

A policy that addresses the problems of illegal immigration to the United States must be grounded in the lives of real people. Americans take their identity seriously. It is an identity that is formed from a life lived in a certain time and place. Illegal immigration threatens that identity and that conception of citizenship. Members of the Minuteman Project believe that a U.S. citizen is more that just a worker and the United States of America is more than just an economy.

Illegal immigrants to the United States are human beings, too, but they are human beings who do not respect the laws nor the culture of the United States. The fact that illegal immigrants are workers or pawns in some greater game to either create more profits or create a North American Union does not absolve them from breaking our laws or abusing our way of life.

Americans cannot expect acceptable solutions to the illegal immigration problem from the open borders lobby or the corporate elites. These groups are addicted to seeing illegal immigrants from the point of view of their own theories. Members of the Minuteman Project are different. They occupy the high ground where there is very little high ground to be found. They ask Americans to consider the human cost of illegal immigration from the point of view of national identity, citizenship and personal responsibility.

[The Minutemen] are American citizens petitioning their government to protect the nation.

Minutemen Demand that the Government Take Action

Seen from this high ground, amnesty for illegal immigrants is not a point of reference for members of the Minuteman Project. For them, amnesty is to U.S. citizenship what counterfeit coins are to money. The corporate elites and the open border lobbyists, however, will give away U.S. citizenship because it means nothing to them.

Eventually, the American people may listen to what members of the Minuteman Project are saying: secure the borders, enforce our laws and become informed about the problems illegal immigration causes. Once this happens, then the American people will abandon their self-serving politicians along with the elites in big business and the open borders lobby to demand a real solution to the problems caused by illegal immigration.

A real solution to the nation's immigration problems will include deportation of illegal immigrants from the United States. Good citizens will settle for nothing less. The fact that neither the left nor the right, neither the socialists nor the capitalists, want deportation of illegals is a sure sign that deportation is part of the moderate solution.

Deportation of illegal immigrants recognizes their humanity, too. By sending illegal immigrants back to where they came and then helping them improve their own society, we treat them as human beings and responsible moral agents, not just as abstract workers.

Members of the Minuteman Project see a threat to our national identity when they look down at the desolate terrain that divides the United States from Mexico. When members of the Minuteman Project ask for secure borders and enforcement of our immigration laws they are doing what is important. They are American citizens petitioning their government to protect the nation.

13

Reasonable People Should Be Suspicious of the Minuteman Border Patrols

Mary Sanchez

Mary Sanchez is an opinion-page columnist for the Kansas City Star.

The volunteer border patrols, or "Minutemen," who seek to root out illegal aliens are led by a man named Jim Gilchrist. Gilchrist has some valid points when he asserts that the Minutemen have merely drawn attention to the problem of illegal immigration that the U.S. Congress has avoided. He also makes sense when he points out that corporations exacerbate the problem by hiring illegal immigrants as cheap labor. But Gilchrist is wrong when he arms volunteer citizens to hunt down illegal immigrants on the U.S.-Mexican border. Gilchrist would be far more effective if he concentrated on educating the public about the illegal immigration problem, instead of taking the law into his own hands. Fortifying the border will not end illegal immigration. People should be suspicious of Gilchrist and his Minuteman project.

Jim Gilchrist could easily be dismissed as a nut. Or as a vigilante. A bigot. A zealot.

As any number of the names he is being called for organizing a monthlong "patrol" of the U.S./Mexico border during April.

The retired California accountant says he is none of these things. He might be telling the truth. And it is impossible to

Mary Sanchez, "A Dose of Suspicion for the Minuteman Project," *The Kansas City Star*, March 3, 2005. Copyright 2005 *The Kansas City Star*. Reproduced by permission.

delve into his soul and decipher true motives. All that can be done is judge Gilchrist by what he says; by what he does.

Gilchrist's effort "The Minuteman Project" has already drawn nearly 700 volunteers who are intent on "securing the U.S. border." An additional 200 people are on a sort of waiting list.

These are people eager to don camouflage gear, camp out and traipse through a part of the border near Tombstone, Ariz. They say their efforts will help the U.S. Border Patrol catch migrants.

The Minuteman Have Some Valid Arguments

Never mind that the Border Patrol doesn't want their help.

Gilchrist admits he is doing it for publicity. He says he wants to draw national attention to the problem of illegal immigration.

This is where Gilchrist makes sense. He says politicians are showing "downright cowardice." He says far too many politicians are willing to look the other way instead of enforcing immigration laws.

He says corporations are greedy and want cheap labor. And, he says the immigrants are not an "invading army," but rather are, "an invading army of refugees." He says they [are] economic refugees who are simply looking for better economic opportunities because few exist in their own country.

Fortifying the border is not the answer. The numbers of illegal immigrants in the United States have actually increased due to such efforts in recent years. That's right, increased.

Gilchrist is exactly on point with these comments. Politicians are fearful of enacting immigration reform.

It was Congress that pretended in the mid-'90s to penalize employers who hire illegal labor. Congress created a giant loophole for those employers.

Volunteer Border Patrols Will Not Stop Illegal Immigration

"I didn't know he/she was illegal," is basically all an employer has to say to get out of trouble.

Many companies do prefer illegal labor because the people are easy to exploit with low wages and unsafe working conditions. And as long as the disparity of wealth and opportunity exists between the United States and Mexico—human nature will try to find a better life elsewhere; even if it means risking your life to cross a desert.

But if Gilchrist wants more understanding for these stated goals; why this method?

Gilchrist's Minuteman Project is akin to hunting down immigrants like prey. He says he has turned away a few people who seemed too cocky, too prone to mood swings or road rage. But when you put the call out for Rambo; don't be surprised when he shows up.

Why organize an event that will likely draw simplistic media coverage of men running around in flack jackets; not nuanced reporting about the problems of immigration?

If Gilchrist truly wants to bring attention to what drives illegal immigration, he should do so. Organize town hall meetings where people can learn the economics behind illegal immigration.

Sure, that is not publicity sexy. But the root of [the] problem is that Mexico is full of people needing better economic opportunities. And the United States is full of opportunity.

Fortifying the border is not the answer. The numbers of illegal immigrants in the United States have actually increased due to such efforts in recent years. That's right, increased.

Illegal immigrants tend to go back and forth across the border, up to the United States for work, then returning back home to their families. But with more surveillance at the border, many people have begun staying longer in the United States.

Ranchers in the area to be patrolled have told Gilchrist that shots might be fired if any Minutemen stray on to private land. Gilchrist says he mostly fears "two types of agitators": People who want violence to occur during the patrols so they can say, "Told you so." And people who think violence is the only solution to decreasing illegal immigration.

So why create a stage that is perfectly suited for both types? Why organize an event that will likely draw simplistic media coverage of men running around in rack jackets; not nuanced reporting about the problems of immigration?

Reasonable people should be suspicious.

14

Volunteer Border Patrols Are Dangerous

Sarah Vowell

Sarah Vowell is a critic and reporter who is best known for her comic observations on public radio's This American Life. *She has written for such magazines and newspapers as* Esquire, GQ, Los Angeles Times, *and* The Village Voice. *Vowell is also a novelist, and, in 2004, was the voice of Violet Parr in the movie* The Incredibles.

The volunteer border patrols who seek to root out illegal aliens are dangerous. The spirit of 1776 has resurfaced in these vigilante groups called "Minutemen," but they are more dangerous than quaint. No one can seriously believe that these volunteers can protect our nation, and they may well end up shooting one another rather than any supposed enemy. The minuteman spirit has also resurfaced in a documentary about a rock band, also called the "Minutemen." Their idealism and sense of humor is a refreshing contrast with the self-important vigilante minutemen, who are little more than adult men playing with guns.

I have a name for it: 1775 disease. The United States of America wasn't born of the pretty words from Jefferson's pen in the declaration signed on July 4, 1776. It was born of anonymous gunfire at Lexington on April 19, 1775. And ever since, we have carried our violent nativity within us like a virus, a virus that lies dormant from time to time only to break out again and again.

We celebrate the Minutemen of 1775. And I'm not saying we shouldn't. I do love a good "Listen, my children, and you shall hear" legend [from the poem "Paul Revere's Ride" by Henry Wadsworth Longfellow]. In fact, my mushy nationalistic heart skipped a beat when an old Minuteman statue, caked in alien goop, made a cameo in Steven Spielberg's "War of the Worlds."

All I'm saying is that there is an inherent pitfall in revering the volunteer militiamen of Lexington and Concord, our beloved raggedy, gun-toting amateurs who defied the powers-that-were. As when today's raggedy, gun-toting amateurs defy the powers-that-be in their honor and someone gets hurt. Timothy McVeigh, for example. Ten years ago, he bombed the federal building in Oklahoma City—on April 19 [1995].

The Minuteman Project

And now—someone alert the C.D.C. (Center for Disease Control)—1775 disease is breaking out in at least 18 states, thanks to the Minuteman Project. What started back in April as a nutty experiment involving armed citizen volunteers patrolling the Arizona-Mexico border to thwart illegal immigration is spreading to non-border states as well. This week Tennessee got its own Minutemen.

The wonderful spirit of the old Minutemen ... can occasionally be ominous when inspiring latter-day gunmen ...

No serious person thinks random guys with guns stalking Niagara Falls or the Rio Grande are going to make the country safer. On the contrary, in addition to all of our other national security worries, Americans now have to fret for the safety of these clowns, who have been condemned by President Bush as "vigilantes." Because, odds are, the only people they'll end up shooting will be one another.

And I say that not only as a namby-pamby liberal writing for the most uppity newspaper in the world, but also as the daughter of a gunsmith, a man who was so persnickety about the very real danger of firearms' tendency to just go off that he practically made my sister and me don hunter orange just to play with squirt guns.

It's worth remembering that no one knows who fired that "shot heard round the world" at Lexington. What probably happened was that one man got nervous and accidentally pulled the trigger on his musket. (Longfellow meant to put that at the end of "Paul Revere's Ride," but he couldn't find a decent rhyme for "uh-oh.")

The Minuteman Spirit Is Best Found in Art, Not Gunfire

The wonderful spirit of the old Minutemen—their amateurish gumption, their do-it-yourself defiance—can occasionally be ominous when inspiring latter-day gunmen, but glorious with regard to art. The police have way too many half-cocked rule-breakers to deal with; pop music, though, can never have enough.

Grown men playing army on the Mexican border? No, thanks.

"We Jam Econo," Tim Irwin's lovable documentary about the lovable 80s punk band called the Minutemen is making the rounds of film festivals and revival houses this summer. It's nice to revisit the hullabaloo of their songs. And watching the bassist, Mike Watt, driving his van around his California hometown, San Pedro, and pointing at Minutemen landmarks is like listening to a fascinating Concord park ranger lead a tour across North Bridge. "We were minute men," Watt says. That's my-NOOT men—a little homemade band, not the slick Redcoats of arena rock.

Watt and the guitarist, D. Boon, are two men Sam Adams could have had a beer with. Their idealism, their humor and decency, is spellbinding. Their friend Nels Cline points out that Boon used so much treble in his guitar as "a political decision"—to distinguish his sound from Watt's bass, like two "sovereign states." Egalitarian timbre!

Then there's the story of their album "Double Nickels on the Dime," a jab at [rock musician] Sammy Hagar's "I Can't Drive 55." Watt recalls, "We said, 'Well, we'll drive 55 and be crazy with the music instead of crazy with the cars.'"

The best part of the film, and the most heartbreaking, is when Watt walks around the park where he met Boon, a childhood friend who died in a car accident in 1985. "I was quite smitten with him," Watt remembers. "He was playing army and he fell out of a tree on me."

As he stares at the very tree, it occurs to me that playing army when you're 13 is fine. Grown men playing army on the Mexican border? No, thanks.

15

A Volunteer Army Is Sufficient to Meet America's Military Needs

Adam Fifield

Adam Fifield is a staff writer at the Philadelphia Inquirer.

In 2006, Representative Charles Rangel called for the reinstatement of the military draft to ensure that as long as the United States was involved in a war, new recruits would come from all strata of society, and not just from the lower classes, who many say are over-represented in today's all volunteer army. The U.S. military, however, prefers a volunteer army to conscription in order to attract a higher caliber soldier and to ensure that only those who want to serve do so. Critics of this policy claim that children of the upper classes are under-represented in the all-volunteer army and that all Americans should join in the war effort. Sacrifice, they believe, should be shared. Opponents claim that if the draft were reinstated, only children of the wealthy would find a loophole, and that the military would find itself burdened by unwilling recruits. Antiwar activists, youths, and the military all agree that an all-volunteer army is the best policy for the United States.

It's hard to imagine that Oskar Castro could find any common ground with the Pentagon.

But one issue has emerged on which the antiwar organizer and the military agree: bringing back the draft is a bad idea.

Raising the specter of conscription [forced military service], even with the intention to deter war, is a grave risk, said Castro, who runs the Youth & Militarism Project, a Quaker-run program that tries to counteract the presence of military recruiters in high schools.

Mandatory service is immoral, Castro said, a practice that is not "consistent with the principles of a democratic republic."

The U.S. military prefers a volunteer force because retention is greater and it attracts a higher-caliber soldier, a Defense Department spokesman said.

Resurrecting the draft, which ended in 1973, has become a hot topic since Rep. Charles Rangel, D-N.Y., pledged to introduce a bill next month [January 2007] that subjects all 18- to 42-year-olds, male and female, to the possibility of mandatory service.

The outspoken critic of the Iraq war says his goal is to force lawmakers to think more about the human cost of going to battle and to spread the burden of service more fairly across the population.

Democratic leaders say the bill, similar to earlier Rangel proposals, will go nowhere. But the congressman is unfazed.

"As long as Americans are being shipped off to war, then everybody should be vulnerable, not just those who, because of economic circumstances, are attracted by lucrative enlistment bonuses and educational incentives," Rangel, a Korean War veteran, said in a statement.

Many Teens Oppose a Military Draft

Among teens, the possibility of a draft has inspired more exasperation than introspection.

It is a "drastic measure to maybe sway a few members of Congress," said Matt Schreffler, 18, who has applied to the U.S. Naval Academy. Schreffler said he would hate as an officer "to lead a bunch of kids who don't want to be there."

"I think if they put the draft in, Bush would use it," said Derek Burkholder, 17.

It makes no sense, said high school senior Bonnie Kelly, 17, who opposes the war: "If there are people who feel strongly, they can volunteer."

Z'Andrea English, 17, a high school senior and ROTC cadet, is not hesitant to serve. She would prefer, however, to stand alongside soldiers who are there willingly.

"If you don't want to be there, you're not going to do your job right," English said. And "if you're not going to do your job right, we really don't need you."

Social Class Is a Major Factor in Who Serves

The Army exceeded its recruitment goal in the just-ended fiscal year. Nonetheless, the Selective Service System maintains a record of potential male draftees 18 to 26. Nationally, 76 percent of 18-year-olds are registered, as required by law, an agency spokesman said.

Rangel, whose Upper Manhattan district includes Harlem and Washington Heights, argues that minorities and the poor carry a "disproportionate burden" in Iraq. His office cites a study by the nonprofit National Priorities Project that found an increasingly disproportionate number of middle- and low-income Army enlistees in 2005 compared with 2004.

The Defense Department disputes Rangel's charge. It offers Heritage Foundation findings that recruits in 2004 and 2005 "came primarily from middle-class areas" and that the volunteer force reflects the race, income and education of the general population.

The military has become more representative in the last 30 years, but children of the affluent are still largely absent, said Temple University professor Beth Bailey, who is writing a history of recruitment and the draft in the 20th century.

"It's not people who have no other options who the military wants or gets," Bailey said. But recruits are rarely "those who are going to the elite colleges, who come primarily from the top 20 percent of income."

Rangel's plan would offer no college deferments, a spokesman for the legislator said.

Putting unhappy people and loaded weapons together is never a sound approach.

ROTC cadet Joshua Dempsey, a high school senior, said he might enlist to attend college, "because my family is not that privileged." While he doesn't think we need it "this second," he is not opposed to a draft.

Rangel's philosophy of equal sacrifice appeals to him. "It should be a shared thing," Dempsey, 18, said.

The Military Draft May Eventually Be Reinstated

Karen Porter of the Chester County (Pa.) Peace Movement appreciates Rangel's larger point, too.

He "knows full well" that his effort will not be what revives the draft, said Porter, who strongly opposes mandatory service.

"What he's trying to do is get the American public to know that if this government doesn't shape up, we're going to be in a situation where it WILL happen."

But Castro, of the Philadelphia-based American Friends Service Committee, fears "a worst-case scenario" in which the bill is eventually passed.

Then the poor and minorities will have no say about their service, Castro said, while "the CEOs of Fortune 500 corporations, their sons and daughters, will find ways out."

High school senior and ROTC cadet Wessley Square, 17, would hate for that to happen.

"Putting unhappy people and loaded weapons together is never a sound approach," he said.

16

The All-Volunteer Army
Is a Failure

Andrew J. Bacevich

Andrew J. Bacevich is professor of international relations at Boston University. He is the author of The New American Militarism: How Americans Are Seduced by War.

Since the end of the Vietnam War, when the United States ended the military draft, enlistment in the armed services has been entirely voluntary. This model served well while the United States was involved only in minor and sporadic conflicts, but in the aftermath of the September 11, 2001 terrorist attacks, the focus of the military changed. U.S. campaigns in Afghanistan and Iraq have severely challenged the volunteer military model. As the war in Iraq turned more unpopular, recruitment became increasingly difficult, and in pursuing the present course of war abroad, the U.S. military may run out of voluntary soldiers. Given this possibility, the United States may either have to reinstate the draft or change its current policy of overseas involvement and only enter into conflicts that the entire nation will support.

The All-Volunteer Force (AVF), arguably the most successful and widely hailed federal program of the past thirty years, is failing. The conditions that enabled the AVF to thrive through the 1980s and 1990s no longer pertain. The erosion of those conditions, greatly accelerated by the Iraq War, is exposing as false the great unspoken assumption undergirding U.S. policy since the end of the cold war, namely, that the United States can enjoy the prerogatives of being the world's sole superpower on the cheap.

Americans will soon confront a fundamental choice: they can continue to pursue a policy of militarized hegemony— currently styled as spreading freedom and democracy across the Islamic world—or they can preserve the practice, adopted after Vietnam, of insulating themselves from the costs that hegemony entails. But they cannot do both.

Ending the Military Draft

Until Vietnam, Americans had traditionally viewed military service, at least in principle, as an obligation inherent in citizenship. Never comfortable with what the Founders had called a "standing army," they had seen the citizen-soldier as the mainstay of U.S. military policy. In times of emergency, Americans rallied to the colors; once the emergency passed, they just as quickly headed home.

The coming of the twentieth century saw efforts to rationalize this process. During two world wars and through the first two decades of the cold war, Americans had conceded to the federal government the authority to determine which citizens would actually serve and in what capacity. For a time, conscription seemed the best way to blend efficacy with fairness.

In retaliation for the government's mendacity and recklessness in Vietnam, though, Americans revoked that grant of authority. Through widespread protest, resistance, and subversion, they brought the then-existing system of Selective Service to a halt. When Richard Nixon formally ended the draft in 1973, he was ratifying what had already become self-evident: as a practical matter, government could no longer command citizens to serve. But, in instituting the All-Volunteer Force, Nixon went a step further; he effectively severed the relationship between citizenship and military service. Serving in uniform became strictly a matter of personal choice.

The New Volunteer Army

Initially, persuading young Americans to make that choice proved to be a tough sell. In the 1970s, love of country had come to be seen as a retrograde sentiment; playing on patriotic themes did not inspire the nation's eighteen-year-olds to march down to their nearest Army recruiter. With the post-1960s cultural mood skeptical of authority and celebrating immediate self-gratification, the prospect of subordination to what was then called "the green machine" exercised limited appeal.

To be all they could be, the affluent didn't need to spend a hitch in the Army or the Navy: they had daddy or, better still, a trust fund.

In the face of these obstacles, the armed services consciously set out to rebrand themselves. They promoted military service as a career opportunity and a path to self-actualization. At a time when high-wage blue-collar jobs were becoming increasingly scarce, enlisting in the military offered some of the best blue-collar opportunities in America. The pay was good, benefits generous, the environment family-friendly. Best of all were the assurances that the company wasn't going to go belly-up or get bought out by the Japanese. In the words of the famous jingle, the military became a place where you could "Be All That You Can Be."

The young people who seized on that opportunity tended to be those for whom opportunities otherwise appeared limited. To be all they could be, the affluent didn't need to spend a hitch in the Army or the Navy: they had daddy or, better still, a trust fund. Members of the predominantly white middle class, focused on attendance at a four-year college as the key to continued upward mobility, likewise saw little reason to enlist. Members of the working class and people of color—above all, African Americans—picked up the slack. To oversimplify only slightly, the AVF of the 1980s and 1990s succeeded for one very large reason: when moneyed America opted out of military service, black America joined up in disproportionate numbers.

This was the dirty little secret of the All-Volunteer Force: its ranks were not even remotely representative of the nation as a whole. At the end of the twentieth century, for example, fully 42 percent of U.S. Army enlisted soldiers were minorities. Although African Americans constitute 12 percent of the nation's overall population, in 2000 they accounted for fully a quarter of the Army's enlisted soldiers and a larger percentage still of the noncommissioned officer corps. For those Americans whose understanding of democracy centered on unencumbered individual autonomy, hiring out the function of national defense qualified as perfectly compatible with contemporary civic ideals. For the minority who clung to the view that democracy ought to entail something more than asserting privileges, the AVF seemed less benign. They saw it as a mechanism for offloading onto a few the responsibilities that rightly belonged to the community as a whole.

Granted, as long as this arrangement worked—that is, as long as the AVF satisfied the nation's immediate military needs—no one much cared about such theoretical matters. And the AVF did work, as long as the model of military service as career opportunity retained its plausibility.

Four years into what the Bush administration describes as an open-ended war, evidence that the AVF has begun to unravel is now incontrovertible.

Throughout the 1980s and 1990s, this remained the case. For as long as the cold war defined national security policy, military life had a pronounced rhythm and predictability: surprises were few; the likelihood of getting killed or maimed appeared remote. Once the cold war ended, however, the United States went on an interventionist binge that sent U.S. troops to Panama, the Persian Gulf, Somalia, Haiti, Bosnia, Kosovo, and elsewhere, though these episodes tended to be either brief or, if protracted, relatively small-scale and low-risk. Until September 11, 2001, military service remained salable as an attractive occupation. As a consequence, throughout the abbreviated post-cold-war era, recruiting stayed fairly strong. Indeed, by the end of the century, most Americans viewed the All-Volunteer Force as permanently self-sustaining.

The Military After 9/11

All of that changed after 9/11. Four years into what the Bush administration describes as an open-ended war, evidence that the AVF has begun to unravel is now incontrovertible. The pipeline of new recruits is drying up. For four of the past five months, the Army—the service bearing the brunt of the fighting in Iraq and Afghanistan—has missed its recruiting goal. For May 2005, for example, the Army reduced its announced target from 8,050 to 6,700 recruits—and still fell 25 percent short. Figures for the Army Reserve and National Guard are equally dismal. For the Marine Corps, also heavily engaged in Iraq, the situation is only marginally better: through the first five months of 2005, Marine recruiters managed to meet their quota only once. Notably, these numbers are down although the Pentagon is easing enlistment standards, throwing more money into advertising, offering signing bonuses of up to $20,000, and pushing more recruiters into the field.

In one sense, the cause of the problem is self-evident: the ongoing insurgencies in Iraq and Afghanistan. The Navy and the Air Force, services with a far smaller commitment to the active war zones, continue to meet their recruiting goals. For young people looking for a decent job and a leg up, becoming a sailor or an airman remains an attractive option.

Viewing service in the U.S. Army or U.S. Marine Corps in such terms no longer makes sense. To be sure, combat veterans from Iraq and Afghanistan continue to reenlist in large numbers, suggesting that those already in uniform find there challenge, camaraderie, and a sense of worth derived from being part of something much larger than self. But kids back on the block (and their parents) are taking a different view. Increasingly, they see military service not as a route to self-improvement but as a ticket to a war zone and a risk not worth taking.

Even if restoring the draft were politically feasible (and in the current climate, it's not) doing so would amount to treating symptoms while leaving the disease untouched.

African Americans, the backbone of the AVF in its heyday, are in the vanguard of those now revising their view. The numbers are telling: whereas in fiscal year 2000, 23.5 percent of all Army recruits were black, in the current fiscal year, the comparable figure is 14 percent. Young African Americans are voting with their feet against President Bush's war.

To the extent that Americans, whatever their class or color, are paying any attention to the current recruiting crisis, that attention stems from the fear that lurking just beyond is the prospect of renewed conscription. The White House, the Pentagon, and most politicians adamantly insist that there will be no draft. A few members of Congress, notably Charles Rangel, an African-American veteran of Korea, call for its revival. Either way, such talk misses the larger problem.

Even if restoring the draft were politically feasible (and in the current climate, it's not) doing so would amount to treating symptoms while leaving the disease untouched. The prospective demise of the AVF matters, not because it increases pressure to conscript but because it casts in sharp relief the larger contradictions besetting U.S. policy. The crisis of the All-Volunteer Force opens a window through which the real issue comes into view.

Will the U.S. Run Out of Soldiers?

President Bush has repeatedly portrayed the present conflict as a sequel to the momentous struggles of the past century. Indeed, in his address to the nation on June 28 [2005], the president essentially endorsed Osama bin Laden's description of the current struggle as tantamount to a third world war. But if the war on terror—or, if you prefer, the campaign to democratize the Islamic world—is indeed of such vital importance, then the burden of fulfilling that mission ought to fall across the full spectrum of American society.

Today that is manifestly not the case. During World War II, for example, movie stars, professional athletes, and the offspring of the famous and the well-to-do—even FDR's sons—found themselves in uniform. By comparison, today's boldface names—with professional football player Pat Tillman as the sole and remarkable exception—remain safely in the cosseted cocoon of privilege. Neither of Bush's military-age daughters, for example, has shown any inclination to participate in her father's war. More and more parents are concluding that the Bush family has it right. Issuing the odd throwaway line from the bully pulpit—as when Bush told the assembled troops at Fort Bragg on June 28 that "there is no higher calling than service in our Armed Forces"—is unlikely to change that.

The problems besetting the AVF suggest that the days of undemocratically conceived and undemocratically implemented national-security policies may be numbered. If he continues on his present course, Bush will run out of soldiers long before he runs out of wars.

Given that prospect, one of two things must happen. Either more Americans, especially the affluent and the middle class, need to ante up their sons and daughters to sustain Bush's war, making the enterprise democratic in substance as well as in its proclaimed purpose. Or, failing that, Americans ought to reassert control of U.S. policy, scaling the nation's purposes to our collective willingness to sacrifice. Either way, the crisis of the All-Volunteer Force may yet prove to be salutary.

Organizations to Contact

The editors have compiled the following list of organizations concerned with the issues debated in this book. The descriptions are derived from materials provided by the organizations. All have publications or information available for interested readers. The list was compiled on the date of publication of the present volume; the information provided here may change. Be aware that many organizations take several weeks or longer to respond to inquiries, so allow as much time as possible.

American Red Cross
2025 E Street NW, Washington, DC   20006
(202) 303-4498
Web site: www.redcross.org

The American Red Cross is a humanitarian organization that helps millions of people each year prevent, prepare for, and cope with emergencies. Volunteers can help in a wide variety of ways, from blood donation to disaster relief.

AmeriCorps
1201 New York Avenue, NW, Washington, DC   20525
(202) 606-5000
e-mail: questions@americorps.org
Web site: www.Americorps.org

AmeriCorps is a network of local, state, and national service programs that brings together tens of thousands of volunteers in intensive service to address needs in education, public safety, health, and the environment. "AmeriCorps members serve with more than two thousand nonprofits, public agencies, and faith-based and community organizations."

American Society for the Prevention of Cruelty to Animals
424 E. 92nd St, New York, NY   10128-6804
(212) 876-7700

Web site: www.aspca.org

The American Society for the Prevention of Cruelty to Animals (ASPCA) was created to fight animal cruelty in all of its forms. The ASPCA's activities include "saving a pet who has been accidentally poisoned, fighting to pass humane laws, rescuing animals from abuse or sharing resources with shelters across the country." The ASPCA's mission is to work toward the day "in which no animal will live in pain or fear."

Global Volunteers

375 East Little Canada Road, St. Paul, MN   55117-1628
(800) 487-1074 • fax: (651) 482-0915
e-mail: email@globalvolunteers.org
Web site: www.globalvolunteers.org

Global Volunteers facilitates participation in volunteer vacations abroad or assistance programs in the United States. Volunteers live and work with those in need on "life-affirming community development projects" for up to three weeks. Global Volunteers supports communities in countries around the world through volunteer teams, project funding, and child sponsorships. Volunteers can serve in a variety of ways, from sponsorship to direct support of local people as a family, group, or individual.

Habitat For Humanity International

121 Habitat Street, Americus, GA   31709-3498
(229) 924-6935
e-mail: publicinfo@habitat.org
Web site: www.habitat.org

Habitat for Humanity International (HFHI) is a nonprofit, faith-based housing organization. Habitat attempts "to eliminate poverty housing and homelessness" from the world, and to make decent shelter a matter of availability for all peoples. This organization invites people of all backgrounds, races, and religions to come together to build houses for families in need. Habitat has built nearly a quarter million houses around the world, "providing more than a million people in more than 3,000 communities with safe, decent, affordable shelter."

Meals On Wheels Association of America
203 S. Union Street, Alexandria, VA   22314
(703) 548-5558 • fax: (703) 548-8024
Web site: www.mowaa.org

The Meals On Wheels Association of America (MOWAA) provides meal services to those in need. MOWAA works toward the social, physical, nutritional, and economic betterment of vulnerable Americans. It funds local senior meal programs throughout the country to provide meals and other nutrition services. Volunteers deliver hot meals to the elderly or disabled.

The Nature Conservancy
4245 North Fairfax Drive, Suite 100
Arlington, VA   22203-1606
(800) 628-6860
Web site: www.nature.org

The Nature Conservancy is a leading conservation organization operating on a worldwide level "to protect ecologically important lands and waters for nature and people."

Points of Light Foundation
1400 I Street, NW Suite 800, Washington, DC   20005
(202) 729-8000 • fax: (202) 729-8100
e-mail: info@pointsoflight.org
Web site: www.pointsoflight.org

"The Points of Light Foundation and Volunteer Center National Network engages and mobilizes millions of volunteers who are helping to solve serious social problems around the United States." Through a variety of programs and services, the Foundation encourages Americans from all walks of life to participate in volunteer activities.

The Salvation Army
615 Slaters Lane, Alexandria, VA   22313
Web site: www.salvationarmyusa.org

The Salvation Army is a faith-based organization providing a diverse range of services through its wide-reaching programs. Volunteers distribute food and support to emergency, fire, and police workers and disaster victims. Volunteers also provide child care, counseling, and media services.

United Nations Volunteers

Postfach 260 111, Bonn   D-53153
   Germany
+49-228-815-2000 • fax: +49-228-815-2001
e-mail: information@unvolunteers.org
Web site: www.onlinevolunteering.org

The United Nations Volunteers (UNV) is the UN organization that supports human development around the world by promoting volunteerism, including the recruitment of volunteers. UNV promotes peace and development through enhancing opportunities for participation by all peoples. It is universal, inclusive, and embraces a diverse range of volunteer activities.

United Way Volunteer Solutions

United Way of America, Alexandria, VA   22314
Web site: www.volunteersolutions.org

United Way Volunteer Solutions is a volunteer matching program that enables individuals to find volunteer opportunities in their communities. "Volunteer Solutions helps volunteers, nonprofit agencies, corporations, event organizers, and Volunteer Centers get connected."

Volunteers of America

1660 Duke Street, Alexandria, VA   22314
(800) 899-0089 • fax: (703) 341-7000
Web site: www.voa.org

Volunteers of America is a national, nonprofit, faith-based organization whose mission is to help the needy rebuild their lives and reach their full potential. Through its numerous and diverse programs, including housing and healthcare, Volunteers of America helps millions of people all over America.

Bibliography

Books

Joshua Achipa, ed.
Volunteerism, Rural Information Center publication series, No. 46. Beltsville, MD: Rural Information Center, National Agricultural Library, 1995.

Barry N. Checkoway and Lorraine M. Gutiérrez, eds.
Youth Participation and Community Change. New York: Haworth Press, 2006.

Melvin Delgado and Lee Staples
Youth-Led Community Organizing: Theory and Action. New York: Oxford University Press, 2008.

Theresa Foy DiGeronimo
A Student's Guide to Volunteering. Franklin Lakes, NJ: Career Press, 1995.

Ronald Eniclerico, ed.
U.S. National Debate Topic 2006–2007: National Service. New York: H. W. Wilson, 2006.

Kathlyn Gay
Volunteering: The Ultimate Teen Guide. Lanham, MD: Scarecrow Press, 2004.

Renée Heiss
Helping Kids Help: Organizing Successful Charitable Projects. Chicago: Zephyr Press, 2007.

Frances A. Karnes and Kristen R. Stephens
Empowered Girls: A Girl's Guide to Positive Activism, Volunteering, and Philanthropy. Waco, TX: Prufrock Press, 2005.

Maureen E. Kenny and Laura A. Gallagher — *Teenagers and Community Service: A Guide to the Issues*. Westport, CT: Praeger, 2003.

Hal Marcovitz — *Teens & Volunteerism*. Broomall, PA: Mason Crest, 2005.

Frank McGuckin, ed. — *Volunteerism*. New York: H. W. Wilson, 1998.

Frank Muschal — *Beyond Government*. Ann Arbor, MI: Cherry Lake Pub., 2008.

Marc A. Musick and John Wilson — *Volunteers: A Social Profile*. Bloomington: Indiana University Press, 2007.

Margit Misangyi Watts — *Service Learning*. Upper Saddle River, NJ: Pearson/Prentice Hall, 2007.

Dan Zadra — *The Heart of a Volunteer*. Seattle, WA: Compendium, 2004.

Periodicals

Al Arends — "Paying it Forward," *Office Products International*, October 2006.

Leslie Barban — "Building Character and Responsibility: A Decade of Junior Volunteers," *American Libraries*, June–July 1997.

Michael Barone — "Faith In Our Future?," *U.S. News & World Report*, April 24, 2005.

Drake Bennett — "Doing Disservice: The Benefits and Limits of Volunteerism," *American Prospect*, September 30, 2003.

Bruce Chapman   "A Bad Idea Whose Time Is Past: The Case Against Universal Service," *Brookings Review*, September 22, 2002.

Paul Clolery   "Bush Touts Faith-Based Answers for Social Services," *Non-Profit Times*, April 1, 2006.

Ad de Raad   "Proactively Embracing Volunteerism," *UN Chronicle*, December 2006.

Jane R. Eisner   "No Paintbrushes, No Paint: The Realities of Volunteer Work," *Brookings Review*, Fall 1997.

Susan J. Ellis   "Newest Recruits; Questioning the Baby Boomer Effect on Volunteerism," *Non-Profit Times*, November 1, 2006.

Susan J. Ellis   "Numbers Game: It's Time to Start Counting Volunteers Seriously," *Non-Profit Times*, February 1, 2006.

Peter B. Gemma   "Looking Up From the Grass Roots: Minutemen Project Represents 'Middle American Radicals' in Action," *Social Contract Quarterly*, Spring 2007.

Michael J. Gerson   "Do Do-Gooders Do Much Good?" *U.S. News & World Report*, April 28, 1997.

Georgie Anne Geyer   "On the Border," *American Legion*, March 2006.

Winston Groom   "An Army of 50 Million? The Sur-
passingly Dishonest Draft Debate,
Weekly Standard, December 11, 2006.

Cathy Gulli   "Kids With a Cause: Some Schools in
Canada Force Students to Volunteer.
Even Then, it Turns Out to Be Good
for Them," *Maclean's*, November 21,
2005.

Nancy Jamison   "The Bottom Line: Corporate Giving
and Sue Carter   Gives Back," *San Diego Business Journal*, May 28, 2007.

Tanya Lewis   "Cover Story: The Art of Giving
Back," *PR Week*, May 7, 2007.

Robert E. Litan   "September 11, 2001: The Case for
Universal Service," *Brookings Review*,
Fall 2002.

Jorge Mariscal   "The Poverty Draft: Do Military Re-
cruiters Disproportionately Target
Communities of Color and the
Poor?" *Sojourners*, June 2007.

John McCain   "Do the Nation a Service," *Newsweek*,
September 15, 2003.

Colman   "A Win-Win Situation: The Real Ben-
McCarthy   efits of Volunteerism," *Washington
Monthly*, June 1997.

Terry McCarthy   "Stalking the Day Laborers: Border-
Patrolling Minutemen Turn Inland in
Their Fight Against Illegal Immi-
grants. What's the Real Goal?" *Time*,
December 5, 2005.

Non-profit Times   "One-Third of Volunteers Dropped Out," *Non-profit Times*, June 1, 2007.

Camille Noe Pagan   "Helping Hands," *Prevention*, January 2007.

Scott Poland   "The Spirit of Giving Is Alive Among Teenagers," *USA Today*, July 2002.

Richard A. Posner   "An Army of the Willing—Why Conscription Does Not Serve Community," *New Republic*, May 19, 2003.

Gracie Bonds Staples   "Quarterlife Crisis: Helping Others Gives Lives Focus," *Atlanta Journal-Constitution*, November 16, 2004.

Walter L. Stewart Jr.   "The All-Volunteer Army: Can We Still Claim Success?" *Military Review*, July–August 2006.

Julie Sulc   "Crossing the Line," *American City & County*, September 1, 2003.

Michael Tanner   "Corrupting Charity," *USA Today*, September 2001.

Stacy A. Teicher   "Corner Office Volunteers," *Christian Science Monitor*, July 19, 2004.

Hannah Wallace   "Sweet Charity: A Few Hours Spent Volunteering to Help Others Can Ease Stress and Improve Your Health," *Natural Health*, April 2007.

J.C Watts and Forrest Church   "Partners: God and Uncle Sam?," *New York Times Upfront*, September 17, 2001.

Index